Leadership Character

Edited by
Richard Leslie Parrott, Ph.D.

ISBN 0-9722933-2-9

"Effective leadership requires a trusting relationship between the leader and his/her followers. Trust is given by the follower and is based, not so much on the reputation or position of the leader, but the fact that the leader has a vision for the future that the follower prefers, an action plan for achieving that vision the follower accepts, and the passion, discipline and confidence to carry out the action plan whatever crisis may develop. A leader serves and empowers his/her followers, is willing to take risks and models his values for followers."

—Emmanuel "Buzz" Sandberg

Contents

Invitation to a Journey introduces the Roundtable of October 2001 and the theme of leadership character. Contributors are:

  Paul Sears
  Fred Finks

  Learning Exercise #1: The Ins and Outs of Leadership

In this chapter, articles by nationally known speakers present leadership character is seen through four lenses: credibility, accountability, integrity, and personal vision. Contributors are:

  Lovett Weems
  Valerie Brown
  Bill Perkins
  Paul Blease

  Learning Exercise #2: Building a Foundation of Credibility
  Learning Exercise #3: Designing a Framework of
                                        Accountability
  Learning Exercise #4: Building the Walls of Integrity
  Learning Exercise #5: If You Climb the Walls, Climb the Right
                                        Walls
  Learning Exercise #6: Making an Appraisal of My Leadership
                                        Character

Chapter 3
Leadership Character: Discovering Your Way   59

This chapter contains the stories and reflections of six leaders on their journey of character development. The contributors are:

LeBron Fairbanks
Marc Farmer
Larita Hand
Mary Kaufmann
Charles Lake
Rod Bushey

Learning Exercise #7:   Stories from the Journey
Learning Exercise #8:   Leadership Development in the Classroom
Learning Exercise #9:   Leadership Development in Your Organization
Learning Exercise #10: Leadership Development from a Biblical Base
Learning Exercise #11: For Personal Leadership Character Development

Chapter 4
The Leader/Teacher: Inviting Others to Share the Trip   87

This chapter explains the principles of being a leader/teacher. The contributors are:

LeBron Fairbanks
Marc Farmer
Larita Hand
Mary Kaufmann
Charles Lake
Rod Bushey

Learning Exercise #12: A Vision for a Leader/Teacher
Learning Exercise #13: Relationships with a Leader/Teacher
Learning Exercise #14: A Support Structure for Developing Leaders

Chapter 7
Traveling Companions: We Need Each Other

Leaders need others to support, challenge, encourage, and motivate them in character development. In this chapter, you will hear from three groups of leaders as they reflect on what they learned from the Roundtable. The contributors are:

Jonathon Dowdy
Jaime Gillespie
Bob Grover
Shawn Oliver
Vickie Taylor
Bob Rosa
Lovett Weems
Valerie Brown
Bill Perkins

Learning Experience #21: What Leaders Learn

Leadership Character

In October of 2001, a group of forty-eight leaders representing business, government, non-profit organizations, academics and the church met for three days at *The Sandberg Leadership Center* on the campus of *Ashland Theological Seminary* to discuss leadership character, especially the qualities of Christian leadership character.

Introduction

October, 2001. A group of forty-eight leaders representing business, government, non-profit organizations, academics and the church met for three days to discuss leadership character, especially the character qualities of Christian Leaders. The twenty presentations and twenty-four roundtable discussions centered on four questions:

What is essential to good leadership character? Authenticity was the group's answer. A good leader must be true to the "inner self," genuine in action and attitude.

What is the major obstacle to good leadership character? Fear was the consensus of the group. Fear can be masked as conceit, busyness, denial, or a volatile personality.

What is the key resource in developing good leadership character? The group agreed that healthy relationships is the key. It is in healthy relationships that a leader can engage passion and find grounding.

What is the key to mentoring others in good leadership character? Trusting the process. Mentoring means shifting the focus off outcomes and concentrating on the process of growth.

As facilitator for the Roundtable, it was my privilege to listen to many conversations and presentations. Those participating in the event

1

held the recurrent conviction that good leadership character is grounded in a personal and deeply spiritual relationship with Jesus Christ.

These leaders report that personal spiritual vitality is the foundation of authenticity. They are convinced that inner wholeness equips a leader to engage personal fear with honesty and courage. They believe that the healthy relationships that help them grow personally are more than just professional, but are deeply spiritual. Finally, these leaders trust the process of growing in Christ rather than manipulating outcomes as a means of mentoring others.

This book is your invitation to join the roundtable discussion. But more significantly, this book is an invitation from all the participants of the Roundtable to join the journey of developing leadership character. It is an invitation that continues the invitation of Christ, *"Follow me, and I will make you..."* (Matthew 4:19)

Appreciation

I want to express my appreciation to the many people who made this Roundtable possible. Thank you, Dr. Fred Finks, President of Ashland Theological Seminary for embracing the vision, providing the resources, and giving of yourself to the project.

Cheryl Schmiedt served as my administrative assistant She gave of herself beyond the call of duty to turn the vision reality. I appreciate her concern for each person and each detail. Cheryl also invested many volunteer hours typing the manuscript for this book.

Dr. Lisa Berlinger, director of PONPO, served as my advisor throughout the process. The facilitators of the roundtable conversations included Vicky Taylor, Shawn Oliver, Bob Rosa, and Pat Foote, as well as Bob Grover, Jamie Gillespie, and Jonathan Dowdy. Shannon Frank prepared the final formatting of the book.

Finally, thank you to all the participants. Each gave quality time, thought, and energy. They are leaders who represent the best in character.

Richard Leslie Parrott, Ph.D. Executive Director
The Sandberg Leadership Center
October 5, 2002

Chapter 1
Leadership Character: Invitation to a Journey

Leadership is the process of influencing others to reach a common goal. Without influence, leadership does not exist. Leaders develop a pattern of behavior that intentionally influences others, always in order to move them toward the accomplishment of the group's goals.

Character is the *"aggregate of qualities that distinguish one person from another"* (American Heritage Dictionary). ." Much of leadership discussion on character is aimed at "moral character. This is particularly true today in light of the number of moral failures and ethical violation in public view. When you speak of a person as having "moral character," they exhibit a pattern or quality of behavior that distinguishes them from an immoral person. We need moral and ethical leaders!

A person of "leadership character" has a quality or pattern of behavior that distinguishes them from people who are not leaders. Leaders display patterns of relating and responding that influence the actions of others. Leadership character is the habit or pattern of behavior that provides good leadership.

If you habitually say one thing and follow through on it, if you habitually stand up for the greater good of the organization, if you habitually reconsider a decision when the situation has changed, if you habitually learn from others, then you are providing a pattern of good leadership – you display leadership character.

However, if you habitually say one thing but do another, if you habitually back down under pressure, if you habitually push ahead with your original plans even when the situation has changed, if you habitually refuse to learn from others, then you are providing a pattern of poor leadership – you lack leadership character.

- What is the pattern of behaving and relating that provides good leadership?
- What is the spiritual foundation of good leadership character?
- How is good leadership character developed?
- How can leaders mentor others?
- How can one develop a personal vision for leadership?
- How is character developed in the daily experience of leadership?

These are the questions discussed at a Roundtable Convocation held at The Sandberg Leadership Center on the campus of Ashland Theological Seminary, October 25-27, 2001. There were 48 participants representing business, government, nonprofit organizations, academics, and the church.

The Plan of the Book: A Journey Toward Leadership Character

This book is your invitation to take part in a continuing journey toward leadership character. Join a band of leaders in an ever-broadening conversation on leadership character.

Mapping Our Way. A discussion of the meaning of leadership character (Chapter 2) is followed by personal stories and reflections set against a framework of five discoveries needed for leadership development (Chapter 3).

Sharing the Path. Great leaders are also great teachers of leaders. In Chapter 4, you will be given an opportunity to examine your own motives and methods for developing leadership character in others. A group of nine leaders probe the heart of leadership in order to help you help others develop a personal vision for leadership (Chapter 5).

The Journey Continues. Developing character is a journey that happens as leaders reflect on their daily work (Chapter 6) and interact with other leaders (Chapter 7).

Each chapter ends with **Learning Exercises** designed primarily for your own roundtable of three to four people. These exercises may be adapted for most organizations, academic settings, or leadership accountability groups.

Also, throughout the book are short quotes, insights **For Reflection**, from the Roundtable participants to inspire you along your journey.

The First Step on the Journey

Let me introduce myself: My name is Richard Leslie Parrott. I am the Executive Director of the Sandberg Leadership Center and will serve as your guide as we take this journey together. I will be introducing each chapter, furnishing a framework for the articles, and providing learning exercises especially for those who teach leadership.

Character is measured externally, but originates in the heart. Character is what followers see in their leader. What they see engenders trust or mistrust. However, for the leader, the battle is internal. It is a struggle to match ones self with one's vocation.

The following brief article by Paul Sears, Dean of the School of Business of Ashland University, delineates the internal and external components of leadership development.

LEADERSHIP CHARACTER
MAKES THE DIFFERENCE IN MY WORK
by Paul A. Sears, Ph.D.

If the learned pattern of effective behavior that defines leadership character must encompass both external and internal change efforts (see my paper on Strengths and Crisis of Leadership Character), then how does one learn to do this? There is still controversy in the leadership studies area as to whether leadership behavior can be taught. Clearly leadership principles can be taught, but can those principles be made tacit and translated into consistently effective *behaviors*?

Many would say "yes". The armed forces, for one. The various branches of the armed forces have invested enormous amounts of resources in creating systems for making officers and leaders out of a significant portion of their recruits. While the military would not argue that everyone can be turned into a leader, they would probably agree that a willing and able recruit with the requisite mental and physical skills can be transformed into a leader through their leadership training and development efforts. Indeed, they regularly bet millions of dollars and even the lives of service people on their ability to do just that.

As the Dean of a collegiate business school, I would bet that schools, colleges, universities and seminaries would probably hedge their answers more than the military. While many of these institutions boast mission statements that claim they create leaders, in fact the primarily educational outcomes on which they focus attention and resources rarely include leadership behaviors per se. While undoubtedly some students at these institutions do develop effective leadership behaviors (for which the schools then try to take credit), these outcomes are not as intentional

8

and predictable as the educational institutions would like to suggest they are.

Finally, many would argue that leadership (particularly the charismatic or transformative form of leadership behavior) cannot be taught but is largely innate, or at least cannot be predictably developed and enhanced by our existing methods of leadership development. But all of these arguments focus on leadership behavior that is primarily external in its focus. Little attention is paid to the notion of leadership or change management with an internal focus.

Except the church. Almost all religions have a "messenger from God" model leader who not only attempts to change the external world and influence people in that world, but who also goes through and models a transformative internal change. Thus the world's religions seem to model the ideal and most effective form of leadership character which is focused on both external and internal change and transformation. This is the strength of leadership character as developed through religious study and vicarious learning.

Leadership character as developed through religious and pastoral study and vicarious learning that defines the "religious approach" to leadership character enjoys only a peripheral role in the scholarly dialogue on leadership. One thread of the leadership dialogue that bridges the secular and religious approaches to leadership is that of "servant leadership". Servant leadership has developed, in part, through a study of Jesus and his leadership style. However, there is also a conscious, even self-conscious, attempt to make servant leadership a secular model of leadership character. Given the strengths of approaching leadership through the study of religion, with its balanced focus on both external and internal change management, it may be time for the religious approach to assert itself into the dialogue on leadership more insistently, especially in light of some of the recent and more dramatic examples of the failure of the secular leadership model at the highest levels of government.

However, business school faculty are often reluctant to employ an approach that combines deep, personal, transformative change with traditional leadership studies. I am not referring to the superficial personal style adjustments suggested by the situational leadership literature, but rather developing a profound sense of personal and organizational mission and vision linked to a unique organizational context and expressing itself in behaviors that are apt and effective in that particular organizational culture.

There are several reasons why business school faculty are reluctant to go down this path. One reason is that most faculty were not trained in a religious or personally transformative context. Their lack of training and perspective on the importance of personal change accounts for a significant part of the disconnect between personal change in leaders and successful organizational change.

But I think business school faculty may hesitate to focus on the importance of personal transformation in part because they are afraid to loose their "expert" status. As content experts, the theories, models and frameworks of the leadership literature provide unending opportunities to demonstrate their expertise. But personal transformation is not a subject that they can easily demonstrate their superiority over their students. Indeed, some of the students may be experiencing college as a personal transformation and possess more experiential data on the subject than their professors.

Finally, faculty seems to be reluctant to prescribe answers or solutions for students, preferring that the student find their own answers. Theories and concepts permit students to do that, but requiring them to change seems too prescriptive. However, some schools are beginning to recognize that the business world is suggesting, even demanding, change. As more and more business schools adopt an "outcomes-oriented, continuous-improvement approach" to accreditation, they are being encouraged to define outcomes in terms that are important to key stakeholders in their environment. And for business schools, the employers and other key players in the business world are obviously key stakeholders.

What these stakeholders are making clear is that integrity and honesty are important student outcomes. As business schools listen more carefully to their key stakeholders, they are being forced to become more prescriptive. Businesses want graduates who possess integrity. Followers want leaders who have integrity. Business school faculty are beginning to respond with information and courses like "Business Ethics". Some schools are even going beyond the expectation that students must know about ethics, to the notion that students must practice ethical behavior.

The concept of leadership character provides a foundation for my own efforts to encourage our faculty to adopt integrity and accountability as competencies in our outcomes-assessment model. We have not reached consensus on this issue yet, but we are moving in the right direction.

> *"Leadership character is not a cloak to put on and take off at will; rather it is an integration of principles woven into the fabric of who we are."* – Bob Grover

Developing character in leadership demand personal vision and self-awareness. It is living in the tension of "what I can be" and "the way I behave." Bridging the gaps means engaging your strengths. It calls for an emerging, flexible plan and healthy relationships. In this article by Dr. Fred Finks, you will read the story of a journey into leadership development.

LEADERSHIP CHARACTERISTICS OF SERVANT LEADERS
by Dr. Frederick J. Finks
President, Ashland Theological Seminary

Seminary was behind me; the future of church ministry lay before. I'm sure that my enthusiasm was no different than anyone else who had waited to get into the action. Four years of college, three of seminary and ordination behind me, I went boldly and courageously into my first full time pastoral assignment. Now thirty years later, I have had much time to reflect on those early years and the way I was shaped in ministry.

At 26 years of age, I didn't have a lot of experience, maturity or expertise to do ministry. I had desire, training, and knowledge, but was yet to be tested in the real world where good and evil intertwined sometimes boldly and at other times indiscernible. It was here that I learned about ministry, leadership and just who I was in the mix.

Winding Waters Brethren Church in Elkhart, Indiana was a blessing to me. I had weighed going on for a Ph. D instead of ministry. As we exited off of the Indiana Toll Road for our first interview my wife,

11

Holly, commented, "I could just as soon go to Texas today." My response was supportive, "Me, too." But what was to unfold in the next couple of days was a congregation that loved the Lord and loved each other and they offered their love freely and abundantly to us.

I can remember my interview with the Board of Trustees. They began by sharing personally about their lives and about their commitment to the church. Then they made what was the one discerning statement that sealed the decision for me. "We are willing to try anything once. If it doesn't work, we admit it and go on." In those words was room for me to succeed or fail. It didn't matter. It was the most freeing words I had ever heard before and since.

Winding Waters was unique in other ways. It was a small congregation of 72. It was only 8 years old having been a church plant in 1964 from a more traditional mother church. The congregation was made up of those who were willing to dream and take risks. It was also a church that was dependent upon one another. It was not wealthy nor was it poor. But within its operating structure, it depended upon volunteers to do ministry. Signs were posted on the church bulletin board and in the Sunday bulletin listing sign up sheets for people to serve in the nursery, clean the church, mow the lawn and shovel the snow. Every few months there was a "work day" where most members showed up to keep the church looking good. It was a *servant church modeling servant leadership*. And unbeknown to me, it was shaping me into a servant leader.

In those early years, I soon discovered that I didn't know everything about ministry. I learned as much from them as they learned from me. Probably more! (Years after leaving I looked back over my early sermon manuscripts and was even more convinced as to how much they loved me by putting up with my preaching). These were the shaping years of my life and my ministry. I was allowed to take risks. I was allowed to fail. I was given the freedom to grow and mature as a leader surrounded by people who loved me and encouraged me.

Today, I am a strong advocate of the biblical model of servant leadership. I was sparked in the early eighties by Robert Greenleaf's book on *Servant Leadership* which was given to me by a colleague at the seminary. I now had a name for the style of leadership that I had seen modeled before me at Winding Waters. It was at the core of who I was and it was what I wanted to be. I was further sparked by a treatise that Greenleaf wrote from his experience as a trustee at a seminary entitled,

The Seminary as Servant. He prodded my spirit when he asked what a seminary would look like if it was a servant seminary.

I am not a true servant leader. I must fight my ego every day. It is waiting for me anxiously when I get out of bed in the morning and it would like to play a dominate role in all my relationships. It is hard to suppress, but most necessary if I am to lead with a servant's heart.

As I have reflected on the characteristics that are most important for a servant leader, I have put them into four categories: Spiritually formed, Spiritually focused, Spiritually directed and Spiritually balanced.

Spiritually Formed

Within theological circles the term spiritual formation has become quite familiar. It is defined as the process of developing and nurturing an intimate relationship with God that encompasses heart, soul mind and spirit. Robert Mulholland has defined spiritual formation as, "the process of being conformed to the image of Christ for the sake of others." *Invitation to a Journey, A Road Map for Spiritual Formation* p. 15 I would only seek a slight modification by adding "and ourselves." Spiritual formation is something we do that enriches our own personal life as well as impacting others.

A true servant leader has an intimate relationship with God. He or she is God-centered at the very core of their being. There is no substitute to this intimate relationship. Without it, the leader is easily detracted and turned inward to the point of relying on personal strength and energy.

Servant leaders must stay connected to the true source of strength that comes from being in the presence of God. Daily nourishment from in-depth study of the word and daily prayer places the focus upon God and not oneself. God speaks to us today. His word is activated in one's life as the Spirit sensitizes us to the message of God. Prayer moves from a "want list" to a yielding to what God wants in our lives. Words are not always necessary. Simply being in God's presence infuses one with purpose and vision.

Henri Nouwen in his book, *In the Name of Jesus*, encourages leaders to rediscover their true identity. "I am telling you all this because I am deeply convinced that the Christian leader of the future is called to be completely irrelevant and to stand in the world with nothing to offer but his or her own vulnerable self."(p.17) For Nouwen, he centers on

13

God's love as the heart for all ministry. He states further, "If there is any focus that the Christian leader of the future will need, it is the discipline of dwelling in the presence of the One who keeps asking us, 'Do you love me?"

Unless the servant leader is deeply connected to God and is constantly infused with his active love there is no way to sustain long term effectiveness in ministry. The well will dry up. The leader will experience burn out. There will be nothing to say. There will be no energy to do. Ministry will come to a screeching halt. The leader will crash and burn.

"Are the leaders of the future truly men and women of God, people with an ardent desire to dwell in God's presence, to listen to God's voice, to look at God's beauty, to touch God's incarnate Word and to taste fully God's infinite goodness?" Nouwen (P. 29-30) This is the essence of being spiritually formed and committed to an intimate relationship with God.

Spiritually Focused

A true servant leader has a strong sense of identity and spiritual giftedness. Once one know who they are in being spiritually formed through a relationship with God, it is easy to discover their true identity. There is in each of us a dichotomy of identity. There is the public and the private person. The two can be vastly different or can mirror similarities. It is when the public and the private diverge that the leader is doomed for failure.

For some, the public image is nothing more than a part that they play in a drama. It is a character that takes on a stage presence and moves in a surreal performance mastering the part expected by the audience. It becomes a game, playing the role while keeping hidden the true identity that lies beneath. The play focuses upon the actor or actress and revolves around their part while reality is moved farther and farther from our senses. The church has witnessed the downfall of too many leaders who have played a role while keeping a private identity hidden.

Servant leaders understand that it is not about them, but about God. There is no room for actors on a stage. There is no place for personal performance. There is no place for true identities to be hidden. Spiritual giftedness comes from God at his discretion and choosing. It is not for building up the one, but the many. It is not for personal

14

recognition, but for edifying the church. Servant leaders are in touch with the real self, understanding the flaws and imperfections along with the power of the presence of Christ. As such, ministry is focused outside instead of turning inward. Recognition of a sense of worth comes not from personal achievement but from what Christ has achieved in them. Servant leaders have a defined sense of purpose that is God centered and are willing to take risks.

Spiritually Directed

Servant leaders are spiritually directed. They have been invited by God to see things as they are, but also as they can be. One of the enduring characteristics of all leaders is that they are called to be a visionary. Vision is a gift from God. It is the ability to see a clear mental image of a desirable future.

Many know how to plan for the future. It involves common sense, preparation and dedication. Vision is more than just planning. Vision sees what God is doing and helps move people to its center. A leader who is a visionary has a good sense of reality as it exists. They understand the current situation, the resources available and the mood of the people. Yet they also envision what could be. Two tasks remain, communicating a clear and articulate description of the future and being able to lead people towards it.

Vision by their very nature can not be complex or detailed, but must remain simple. When God showed Abraham the stars in the sky, he said Abraham's descendents would far outnumber them. He didn't go into detail. Likewise with Moses when God told him he would set his people free, he didn't go into detail about the plagues or wilderness ahead. He kept it simple and inspired them to move beyond their own imagined abilities to trust the inspired vision he held before them.

Servant leaders are in touch with God. They are sensitive to his presence. They dream dreams and see visions.

Servant leaders are good communicators. They are able to articulate the vision in a language in which people can clearly understand. They are able to lift and inspire them to move from the mundane into the spectacular, from the routine to the extraordinary. Visions inspire people to do things they can't do alone. Visions inspire people to become part of something much larger than themselves. It helps them refocus on the possibilities instead of the impossibilities. Visions offer hope and a leader who can communicate a hope and a future can inspire people to reach for hidden potentials that have before gone untapped.

People want to be part of something that is larger than themselves. They want to do something that will make a difference. Often times they are restricted from taking risks by their own lack of imagination. But once they are shown a glimpse of what could be, and inspired to become part of it their willingness to risk is enhanced. Sometimes all that it takes to be courageous is to know that those standing next to you are willing to believe the impossibility may just be possible.

Spiritually Balanced

Balance is one of the most important elements for effective leadership. Leadership that is out of balance can not only be ineffective, it can be destructive. For servant leaders balance is enhanced through the development of a shared approach to leadership. Servant leadership sees leadership from the bottom up. In 1978, Donald Karybill described it as *The Upside Down Kingdom.* Most recently in 1999,Greg Laurie's describes it as *The Upside Down Church.* Both capture the essence of Christ's admonition to his disciples that his kingdom would be different, "You know that the rulers of the gentiles lord it over them, and their great men exercise authority over them. It is not so among you, but whoever wishes to become great among you shall be your servant, and whoever wishes to be first among you shall be last." Matthew 20: 25-27.

Servant leaders are people who share decision-making. Terms such as collaborative process and consultative process capture the spirit of shared decision making. Leaders are often called upon to make the final decisions as it affects an organization. The process of shared decision making allows for shared intelligence and shared ownership of the decision to be made and finds ground for empowering individuals to use their spiritual gifts for the common good.

Servant leaders are quick to share credit, quick to praise and slow to accuse. When the emphasis for success is removed from the person and placed where it belongs within the organization, credit empowers and accusations lose their power. On the other hand, when leaders require personal recognition for their successes, giving praise to others becomes almost non-existent. And likewise, failure often requires that others are blamed for the inadequacies.

Servant leaders understand the value of persons and are able to bring balance between tasks and persons. People are not viewed as objects that can be manipulated or coerced for some purpose espoused by the leader. Rather, servant leaders see themselves as responsible for the personal growth and develop of those they serve. Greenleaf defines the test for servant leadership as "Do those served grow as persons, do they, *while* being served, become healthier, wiser, freer, more autonomous, more likely *themselves* to become servants?" Henri Nouwen puts it this way, "Here we touch the most important quality of Christian leadership in the future. It is not a leadership of power and control, but a leadership of powerlessness and humility." P. 63

Servant leadership often runs counter to both the culture of the world and of the church. Not many are willing to lead from the bottom up. Not many are willing to lead by serving. Upward mobility, gaining influence and power become stumbling blocks to effective servant leadership. Servant leadership is not easy, but it is biblical.

Learning Exercise #1:
The Ins and Outs of Leadership

Read the article by Fred Finks, President of Ashland Theological Seminary. In the article, he traces his own leadership development across several decades. After reading the article, discuss with a small group:

- What were the external challenges he was facing; what were the internal changes taking place?

- What are the external challenges you are currently facing in your leadership; what internal changes do you need to embrace?

- To what degree would you concur with the author that servant leadership is the character quality needed by leaders? Are there exceptional situations when servant leadership won't work?

- The author is convinced that character development and personal spirituality are inextricably bound. How does your personal spirituality impact your leadership character?

Chapter 2
Leadership Character: Mapping the Territory

This chapter introduces the subject of leadership character through the writings of four nationally known speakers. Each will present leadership character through a different lens: credibility, accountability, integrity, and personal vision.

A leader who consistently demonstrates quality of character is reciprocated with followers who place trust in their leader. Trust is *"firm reliance on the integrity or ability of a person"* (American Heritage Dictionary). Lovett Weems reflects the significance of trust in the leader.

"TRUST—THE FOUNDATION OF EFFECTIVE LEADERSHIP"
Lovett H. Weems, Jr.
President of Saint Paul School of Theology
in Kansas City, Missouri

We must be the change we seek to produce--Gandhi

Seminary presidents spend much time raising money. Years ago I heard the statistic that large gifts tend to come after a dozen or so visits, often by the president. I was close to that statistical average with a woman in her nineties. She had ample resources, no family, close ties to the church, interest in our school, yet had never given a single gift. I scheduled yet another visit with her by scheduling a flight with a lengthy layover in her city so I could take her to dinner, as was our usual pattern.

When I arrived at her home, she was not dressed to go out. She indicated that she was not feeling well and perhaps we could visit for a few minutes and then I could head back to the airport. We talked briefly in her living room. Then, as we were standing at the door as I was leaving, she said simply, "I trust you." I knew then that we would receive a major gift. She left half of her estate to the seminary for student scholarships.

That was the day I learned that the term "development" was no mere euphemism for "fund raising." It became abundantly clear to me that people give out of trust and that trust grows out of relationships and experience that engender such trust.

When church leaders begin reading supposedly secular books about leadership, it is often a great surprise that the language used in the best of the books seems to come from the vocabulary of the church. Church leaders may expect to find elaborate grids, schemes, and designs. Instead, the words that dominate have to do with values and character. It soon becomes quite evident that there is no way to talk about leadership without talking about values, meaning, character, and relationships.

A term sometimes used in communication theory is the "ethical proof" of the speaker. "Ethical proof" refers to the credibility that the hearers accord the speaker. When the ethical proof is high, the task of persuading the audience is not hard. When the ethical proof is neutral, the speaker has a more difficult time. When the ethical proof is extremely negative, the speaker has a very difficult time persuading the audience. This concept means that the way the constituents perceive the leader is probably much more important than the "facts" of the presentation.

So it is with the presence of trust and credibility between leaders and constituents. James Kouzes speaks of credibility as "credit-ability." People are doing an analysis of our credibility all the time just as a bank might assess our credit worthiness. Indeed, credibility is the working capital of the leader. It is from the account of credibility that the leader draws to make possible creative change. Credibility is the foundation upon which all effective leadership builds.

A leader's trust is won very slowly, but it can be lost quickly. Once lost, this trust is very difficult to regain in that leadership setting.

People may give us a leadership position through election or employment. However, the credibility needed to lead must be worked out among the people with whom we serve. It is trust from those with whom the leader works most closely that gives a leader the essential element of credibility.

Trust Required for Leadership

The level of trust that exists within an organization and toward leaders is crucial to the effectiveness of leadership. When trust is limited, it is difficult for progress to take place. Change requires a minimal level of trust. Some speak of a "trust threshold" or a "radius of trust." That describes the variations in trust we all experience in relation to individuals and groups. Over time we come to extend more trust to some people and organizations than to others.

Economists remind us that in societies where the "radius of trust" is limited to family and a few close friends, a strong and expanding economic life is difficult to achieve. Economic transactions require a certain level of trust. Lack of sufficient trust imposes a kind of tax on all interactions that makes progress more difficult.

This helps explain why in low trust organizations, even modest change is hard to achieve. Conversely, in places where a high level of trust has been developed, remarkable change can be accomplished with a minimum of acrimony and delay.

Components of Trust

Relationships

Warren Carter, who teaches New Testament at Saint Paul School of Theology, describes characteristics that are central to leadership in the Church in the New Testament, and names "relationships" as the first. Helen Doohan notes personal involvement with the people as a significant characteristic of Paul's leadership. It is seen in Paul's early leadership as described in I Thessalonians and developed more fully in later letters in which he is personally and intimately involved with the community, and his life is intimately bound together with theirs. [*Leadership in Paul*, Michael Glazier Publisher, 1984, 59]

It was relationships that provided the foundation for Paul to address pivotal issues. Relationships are more than ends in themselves for leaders. For Paul, involvement and relationship provided a context in which issues and questions could be placed and handled. (*Leadership in Paul*, 59) Relationships are built so that we can all better serve a common mission and vision. On the other hand, working on fulfilling a common purpose, with all its struggles, can be important in building strong and lasting relationships. One does not build positive relationships as a substitute for mission but to make mission possible. And on the way to fulfilling mission, new and even deeper relationships are discovered.

Before there are plans and programs, human relationships must be formed. Credibility is built on relationships. While leaders normally can expect some basic acceptance from the group because of the leadership role, that is not an adequate relational basis for leadership at all. A strong bond must be established if leadership is to take place.

In fact, Kouzes and Barry Posner define leadership as "a reciprocal relationship between those who choose to lead and those who decide to follow." [*Credibility*, 1] Margaret Wheatley makes clear the importance of relationships in her understanding when she says, "Relationships are everything." [*Leadership and the New Science* video]

The first imperative for establishing and maintaining trust is the quality of relationships that are established by the leader. Therefore, the priority for a leader is to establish a relationship of trust and respect with the people with whom the leader is working. Everything depends on this bonding. Relationships are crucial. We come to trust people we know. Building such relationships requires active presence. Absence does not "make the heart grow fonder" in organizational life. Just the opposite. Since we come to trust people we know, whom do we know? We know people who are *there*. Proximity is the most important reason people talk to each other. Leaders are present and visible.

At the most basic level, we trust those who care about us. We trust those who we believe understand our concerns and will act in a way that takes our needs into account. Trust develops from relationships that engender confidence and mutual respect. It is developed within the context of leadership in the day by day interactions with real people in actual circumstances. Proverbs says that "when the righteous are in authority, the people flourish." [Proverbs 29:2] Paul speaks of authority being used for "building up" and not for "tearing down." [II Cor. 13:10] Do people perceive us as caring about them and seeking what is best for them?

22

"Whom you would change," Martin Luther King, Jr., said, "you must first love." Secular writers make the same point in saying "just possibly the best-kept secret of successful leaders is love." [Kouzes and Posner, *The Leadership Challenge*, 305]

Integrity

A second imperative for trust is integrity. Integrity here means honesty and consistency between one's words and actions. Behavior is the key to credibility. Even perceptions of inconsistency hurt trust. Perfection is not the issue so much as coherence among words, values, and actions. Do people see us doing what we say we are going to do?

For a number of years, a United Methodist pastor served in Mississippi with great difficulty. He and his family moved regularly from one modest pastorate to another, sometimes after only one year. The reasons for the frequent moves were many. The educational, personal, and social differences between pastor and assigned congregations were gigantic. However, never far from the surface of parish conflict with their pastor was a profound witness by the pastor against the segregation and racism of the day.

When the United States Supreme Court rendered a decision in late 1969 that finally instituted unitary school systems across the South, this pastor was serving a white congregation in the Mississippi Delta where pronounced African American population majorities are common. The pastor's community was in a school district affected by the ruling. Within a matter of weeks, whites left the public school system with the exception of the pastor's children.

A committee from the church made an appointment with the United Methodist bishop to talk about their pastoral appointment for the coming year. Bishops were accustomed to meeting with delegations upset with this particular pastor. However, the bishop was surprised by the delegation's message. They said, "We don't agree or understand what our pastor and his family are doing. However, we respect his commitment to his beliefs. We understand, bishop, that it may be best for our pastor's family to move. But, we want you to know that our request to you is that our pastor whom we respect be returned for another year."

Personal leadership and organizational leadership require the persistent example and power of integrity. A study of exemplary leaders among Catholic health systems found a "profound synthesis of values and actions." Integrity strengthens the capabilities of leaders and institutions to address pressing needs. As Rosita de Ann Mathews puts it, "Integrity builds structures that become impervious to demonic penetration." ["Using Power from the Periphery," in *A Troubling in My Soul*, ed. by Emilie M. Townes, Orbis, 1992, 101]

Competence

A third imperative for trust is competence. Can constituents depend on the leader's faithfulness in accomplishing what they have a right to expect from their leaders? Are leaders servants of the vision of the group? People may have warm feelings for a leader, but if they are consistently disappointed in the leader's accomplishment of basic expectations, trust will soon evaporate. People may trust the honesty of a leader, but if the leader is not addressing effectively the current needs, trust will not remain strong.

A study of outstanding leaders in nonprofit organizations found that professional competence was essential to their success. [Nanus and Dobbs, *Leaders Who Make a Difference*, 231-232] Likewise, a study of very large congregations found that their pastoral leaders " establish their authority or right to lead not primarily by virtue of the office they hold or because of their formal credentials, but more by a combination of *demonstrated competence* and *religious authenticity*." [Jackson W. Carroll, *Mainline to the Future*, Westminster John Knox Press, 2000, 86, italics added]

Note that the competence required is not technical competence of a type that might be judged and ranked by tests. Rather, the need is for applied competence that assesses what is most needed for a particular time and place and a willingness to assume responsibility for leading people to move in appropriate directions. "Stewardship begins," according to Peter Block, "with the willingness to be accountable for some larger body than ourselves – an organization, a community . . . It requires a level of trust that we are not used to holding." [Peter Block, *Stewardship*, Berrett-Koehler, 1993, 6]

Leaders of character are willing to do what is required, to accept responsibility for faithfulness to mission, to pursue an appropriate vision, and to maintain the healthy functioning of the group. Such leaders guide groups in making decisions to enhance mission and to admit mistakes and change direction when necessary.

Everyone suffers when leaders never get seriously focused on what is most needed by the group and never see themselves as accountable to the group or for the results of the group. Warren Carter captures this sense of appropriate action in the New Testament when he talks about action (doing something) and mission (a community sent out) as constitutive of early church leadership.

Competence illustrates that personal authenticity is not enough. Authenticity and fitting action must come together. Being and doing cannot be separated in understanding character.

When I was in high school, our football team went two years with only one win. To make matters worse, this dry spell came after many years of superior teams under the leadership of a coach who had left. My father was a member of the school board when the superintendent recommended after the second failed season that the current football coach be dismissed. The board members knew a change was needed, but firing someone is never easy. One board member who attended the same church as the coach said, "I hate to see us let him go because he is such a good man." Bringing a sense of reality back to the group, another school board member replied, "My mother was a good woman. But she was no football coach." The board made a coaching change.

Leaders should always be concerned with the question, "What should I be as a person?" They must also keep before them the other question, "What should I be doing?"

Garry Wills maintains that most leadership literature is unitarian when it should be trinitarian. "Unitarian" leadership focuses on the leader. "Trinitarian" leadership has the leader as the "one who mobilizes others toward a goal shared by the leader and followers. . . . Leaders, followers, and goals make up the three equally necessary supports for leadership." (*Certain Trumpets: The Call of Leaders*, Simon & Schuster, 1994, 17)

Leaders come to be seen not as persons pursing their own agendas but as, in the words of Robert Greenleaf, servants of a vision and always seeking a better one. Such leaders of character keep pointing everyone toward the overall mission and calling all to find their place in the fulfillment of a mission far greater and grander than any individual.

Trust Becomes Leadership Through an Inspiring Vision

If trust consists of relationships, integrity, and competence, then inspiration is the ingredient that transforms such trust into effective and compelling leadership. There must be something that distinguishes leadership from mere moral and competent management. Great leaders exude energy and passion for a cause greater than themselves.

Warren Carter speaks of leadership in the New Testament representing an alternative community to the conventional wisdom of its society. Christian community was not the same as the world around them. This was not a separatist model. Indeed, Christians lived in the cities and used language and cultural symbols of their time. However, they were also very different. Their commitment to a vision larger than that of the world made all the difference in their lives.

Such is always the case with leadership of character. Such leaders lift up the "not yet" of God's preferred future and inspire others to make the sometimes difficult journey to the fulfillment of the alternative vision. Leaders do more than manage the circumstances they inherit. They understand that leadership is about pointing to that "land that never has been," in the words of Langston Hughes.

Descartes understood what finally motivates humans. "The passions are the only advocates," he said, "that always persuade." Such passion does not come so much from a leader eliminating all the difficulties faced by people. Indeed, both biblical and secular history remind us that passion comes from a deep and abiding belief that one is a part of something truly important, despite the sacrifices and suffering that often accompany such a journey.

Craig Dykstra's term "visional ethics" captures the interrelationships of vision, action, and character. "For visional ethics, action follows vision," says Dykstra, "and vision depends on character . . . ." (*Vision and Character,* Paulist Press, 1981, 59)

No Character Exemptions for Leaders

The setting for William Golding's novel *The Spire* is a fourteenth century English cathedral town. The dean of the cathedral, Dean Jocelin, has a dream of doing a wonderful thing for God. He sets out to build a four-hundred-foot spire on the cathedral church as a testimony to the

26

greatness and grandeur of God. Surely if he and the congregation can do this great thing, they will serve God well.

Problems emerge from the beginning. The congregation does not share the vision. For that reason the congregation becomes divided. Furthermore, the building will not structurally support such a spire. The builder takes on this project after threats and intimidation. The unwise construction jeopardizes his professional reputation. The construction disrupts church services. Workers die in construction accidents. The pastor takes tainted money to keep the project going. The builder becomes involved with the caretaker's wife. She dies in childbirth having his child.

Through everything, Dean Jocelin persists. After all, he is doing a great thing for God. As the novel unfolds, one sees a spire going steadily upward. At the same time there is human suffering and death caused by the project piling up beneath it. Fulfilling this great dream of Dean Jocelin proves to be extremely costly. It is as if his religious dream has blinded him to all other competing values.

Finally, Dean Jocelin no longer can remain oblivious to what is happening around him. He comes to himself, realizes what has happened, and says with sadness, "If I could go back, I would take God as lying between people and to be found there."

Dean Jocelin should remind us that no vision—no matter how grand, how spiritual, how religious--frees a leader from the trust and character people have a right to expect from leaders.

For Reflection...

"I have been reminded today that as I raise up leaders on the staff of our congregation I need to support and sustain them so that they and I can grow in integrity, authenticity and effectiveness, "to what is God calling us."—Sanford Mitchell

Leaders need support structures that protect and validate the trust

placed upon them. Valerie Brown shared a wonderful, biblical

illustration focusing on financial trust. Read the story and consider the

27

question, "How can a leader build systems and structures that protect and

validate trust such as 'being honest' and 'keeping promises'?"

UNDERSTANDING LEADERSHIP CHARACTER
Valerie K. Brown, CPA
Executive Director and founder of the Church Financial Management
and Leadership Institute, Assistant Professor of Management at the
Samuel D. Proctor School of Theology

If anyone could have accurately identified *the* trait and quality of
an effective leader and put them in a single book, there would be no need
for the hundreds of books that are currently available trying to answer the
questions posed for this convocation on leadership. Peter Drucker, in
Your Leadership is Unique, best sums up this point by saying a major
lesson he has learned after working for over fifty years with leaders is
that there is *no one* leadership personality that will readily ensure that an
individual will be successful as a leader. Yet, after so many years of
studying leaders, their behaviors, qualities, skills, talents, and other
attributes, we are still having leadership as a subject of major interest.
That is because according to Jack Hayford, in *Pastor's Heart,* indicates,
"just about everybody admits leadership {in the church} is needed—now
and most people are fed up with the fake ideas and shallow notions about
leadership."

He says, "we've learned too painfully that position, prominence
and public notoriety are no substitute for *character.* Within the church
we have a brilliant cast of colorful, creative personalities, who also
abound in academic genius refined at institutions that sharpen scholarly
skill while enshrining intellectual acumen. But few of these—platform
stars or mental giants—seem to answer the need for the call for
"leadership." (Hayford, p 1)

Based on Hayford's quote, churches lack good leaders because
of their lack of character; not skills, talents, or education/knowledge
about the Bible. However, research done by Daniel Conway, entitled *The
Reluctant Steward,* concluded that even clergy who have received formal
education at seminaries admit they lack leadership skills and acumen
(without even moving to their character). Conway's research focused on
a survey to identify the extent to which seminaries offered courses in the
areas of leadership....and management to assist clergy in the role leading

28

faith-based entities. (Conway, p. 99) The results showed that many of the theological schools were not "uniformly supportive of the idea that seminaries *should* teach church leaders about leadership" and less than half of the clergy were not satisfied with their ability and skills in this area. (Conway, p. 100)

This paper will present for discussion a summation of research done by several authors. These authors studied character and education and the impact they have on the various types (since there is no one type) of leadership dynamics that are needed for the church of the twenty-first century in order to answer the call to leadership. The paper will focus on addressing the following questions raised for this convocation:

- What is the pattern (or patterns) of behavior that provides good leadership?
- What is the relationship of good ethical, good moral, and good leadership character? (Or does ethics and morals matter?)
- What is the personal foundation for good leadership character?
- How is good leadership character developed?
- How can a leader mentor others in developing good leadership character?

What is the relationship of good ethical, good moral, and good leadership character? (Or does it matter?)

One of many current debates is whether an individual's ethics and moral behavior or character should be considered when analyzing their leadership abilities. True character or behavior is often quoted as "what you do or say when no on can see you." Your true character is who you *really* are; not who you pretend to be. So although Hayford insists that *character* is the missing ingredient in the leaders of the church today, we must explore the use of *character* as defining leaders.

Without taxing our memory too much, one can easily remember the debates that took place over President Bill Clinton and his ethics and moral behavior {or lack thereof}. Leaving party politics out of the discussion for just a moment, the debates went back and forth as to whether President Clinton was fit to serve as President because one assumption was that the person and his ethics and morals were inseparable. In the end, President Clinton was able to "weather" that storm and serve out his remaining term. This was not the case for Rev. Jimmy Swaggert or Rev. Henry Lyons who displayed the same ethical and moral standards of Bill Clinton. Both Rev. Swaggert and Rev.

Lyons were the leaders of major ministries with wealth, prominence, position, and fame the same as Bill Clinton. All were considered great leaders until the discovery of their ethical and moral stance.

But what was the difference in the two scenarios? Do we as a society hold secular leaders to a different standard than our spiritual leaders? Do we define leadership differently given the context of the situation? And if so, what becomes the deciding factor... the position or the trait or quality? If it is the position, then what we are saying is that we do not value ethics or moral behavior (character) as a necessary trait in leaders. If it is the trait or quality that counts, then it should not have mattered what position the individual leader held.

There are also numerous examples of financial mismanagement, misappropriation and theft that have occurred in ministries. The media has reported thefts ranging from the $2 million dollar theft by an Episcopal church treasurer to $750,000.00 from a Methodist priest. There are no denominational differences when it comes to poor internal controls over the financial affairs of the church. Theft and misappropriation is being is occurring among all the levels of leadership within the church. Far too often the church relies on simple trust of the leadership when it comes to the financial affairs. While trust is a character trait one should certainly have prior to accepting a position of leadership while handling the finances of the church, it is not enough to reliable solely upon for the safekeeping of the assets of the church. Trust is lifted up as the paramount character trait for leaders in the church, yet, we find violations of trust everyday. The Bible teaches us that we are our brothers' keepers. We find in the Word of God in the book of Ezra, an example of how the church can become the "brothers' keeper" of the financial officers by instituting checks and balances. In Ezra 8:24-26 we find these words:

"I appointed twelve leaders of the priest to be in charge of transporting the silver, the gold, the gold bowls, and the other items that the king, his council, his leaders, and the people had presented for the temple of God. I weighed the treasure as I gave it to them and found the totals to be..."

This passage was written during the rebuilding of the Temple. People and leaders gave money to the priests for the rebuilding of the Temple. The people surely "trusted" the priest and other workers in the Temple, yet they still counted what was given to the priest prior to giving it to them. The priests were required to transport all that was given back to Jerusalem. Later after the journey to Jerusalem we find in Ezra 8:33:

"On the 4th day after our arrival the silver, gold, and other valuables were weighed at the Temple...everything was accounted for by number and weight and was officially recorded."

The priests were held 'accountable' and there were checks and balances put in place to ensure that the priest were not even tempted to misappropriate or steal any items entrusted in their care. In some churches, individuals feel they are not trusted if they are asked to accurately report or account for items entrusted in their care. This however, is a biblical standard as illustrated through Ezra.

Most ministry failures can be traced to a failure in *character development*; not to a failure in ministry skills or a lack of knowledge. (Easter, p2)

What is the personal foundation for good leadership character?

The personal foundation for good leadership character is for leaders "to become intentional about their *character* growth and formation." (Easter, p 2) The leader must desire to grow and acknowledge their weaknesses and work on them consistently.

Dennis Easter, in *The Healthy Pastoral Leader*, makes three general observations about leadership character development:

God develops a leader over a lifetime

Leaders must recognize that all of their experiences in life will factor into the person that they become and the character they develop. Leaders must assess and learn from each of life's experiences.

God uses people, circumstances and ministry assignments to shape the life of a leader; and

Leaders must accept the fact the people and their environment have a major impact on them, either negatively or positively. Leaders must always, therefore, be on guard about the people and environment in which they surround themselves

Leadership plateau is often indicative of a growth issue within a leader's life.

Leaders sometimes feel stagnated or at an impasse. Leaders rather than feeling lost should take this opportunity to assess where they are, where they are going, and where they have been. Growth normally comes in spurts, with appropriate levels of rest in between.

How is good leadership character developed?

Easter raises five insights for development of leadership character.

Leaders are lifelong learners through informal training and formal training

Leaders know that "they never know it all." Leaders will always look for workshops, continuing education courses, degree programs, or simply personal research projects that continue to expand their mind and character to reach new heights of awareness.

Leaders are committed to serve and develop others by being alert to other potential leaders

A good leader always works himself out of a job by delegating tasks and training others to move ahead in their own personal growth.

Leaders have a dynamic view of life and ministry through purpose, values, and vision.

Leaders do not look at what they do as a job. Leaders *love* their work. Leaders have a *passion* for their work. Their work is their life and there is a purpose behind everything they do.

Leaders experience repeated times of renewal through intimacy with God incorporated with spiritual discipline.

As the spiritual leader of a church or other faith-based entity, the leader must acknowledge God in all that is done and said. This can only be accomplished through a disciplined life of prayer and study of the Word of God.

Leaders have a lifetime perspective.

Leaders rarely ever mention anything about retirement; because for most leaders their work is their life, it is never ending

What is the pattern of behavior that provides good leadership?

As discussed earlier, there is no *one* best pattern of behavior for good leadership. Different situations cause for different patterns of behavior in a leader for the twenty-first century. Those leaders who are unable to quickly adapt their leadership styles to the situation will not be successful. Skills, talents, and traits needed of an individual operating in corporate America in the twentieth century will be totally different for that same individual in that same company in the twenty-first century.

The same is true for clergy who were "successful" leading their congregations a few years ago but now they are finding it increasingly difficult and challenging to lead using those "same old methods, the same old way." According to Lewis in his book, <u>Transformational Leadership</u>, a study of successful leaders show that all these leaders did not possess the same traits and any attempt to analyze leadership by traits have been unsuccessful. While research has uncovered a "list" of attributes commonly possessed by leaders, research concluded that traits demanded of a leader vary from one situation to another. Leaders who are successful in one situation may be unsuccessful in another situation given the type of leader needed for each incident. Lewis identifies several different leadership styles or patterns of behavior as follows:

Situational Leadership --this type of behavior matches the style to the incident. For example, "A group with a high need for control and direction should not be saddled with a democratic leader. A mature, well-functioning group should not have an autocratic leader." Knowing the type of leadership needed in the given situation is the key to the success of the entity.

Visionary Leadership – "is an expression of faith and hope" This type of leader fixes his gaze on goals that may seem impossible to others, yet can paint a picture that compels others to join him in achieving the goal. Most churches and even secular companies desire their leaders to *always* have "vision". However, having a "vision" will not be enough without being able to move the vision from vision to reality.

Possibility Leadership – "Occasions are rare; and those who know how to seize upon them are rarer" This type of leader focuses on the opportunities. They are sometimes known as the "positive thinking" leader; optimistic. However, opportunity alone is not enough; nor is ability. The possibility leader knows how to combine abilities and *seize* opportunities when they present themselves.

Initiatory Leadership – "Between the great things we cannot do and the small things we will not do, the danger is that we shall do nothing." (Adolpe Monod, Lewis, p. 51) Initiatory leaders have the fortitude to begin and the perseverance to follow through. There are many leaders who can begin a project only to allow distractions remove his focus on the goal. While there are other leaders, perhaps, visionary leaders, who can see the goal, but can never get started on the project.

As Maxwell and Lewis have both indicated, leaders need to be flexible and perhaps a little of all these styles given the situation in order to be successful.

In addition to the style or behavior of leaders, according to Lewis (p.207) most leaders at least *think* alike. Here are general statements that Lewis has found to be true of successful leaders.

- Leaders are more concerned with achieving success than avoiding failure. *"The way to succeed is to double your failure rate."* Thomas J. Watson, IBM founder

- Leaders prefer situations they can influence and control rather than outcomes that depend on chance.

- Leaders are future-oriented and can wait on outcomes expected to yield positive results.

- Leaders have a long-standing pattern of working hard to be at the top of their chosen profession.

- Leaders must be willing to take risks. *"Only those who dare to fail greatly can ever achieve greatly."* Robert Kennedy

- Leaders are motivated by their love for God and humanity.

How can a leader mentor others in developing good leadership character?

> *"No man will make a great leader who wants to do it all himself or get all the credit for doing it."*
>
> Andrew Carnegie

Leaders must be able to spot other *potential* leaders. In identifying other potential leaders, current leaders must mentor and develop them. As previously stated, a good leader will work himself out of a job.

According to Fred Smith, in *Spotting a New Leader,* there are ten signs to finding a potential leader:

Leadership in the past- have they held leadership positions, however small, in the past?

The capacity to create or catch the vision- do they show the same enthusiasm you show for the work...can they see what you see?

A constructive spirit of discontent - leaders are never satisfied with status quo. Leaders are always looking for ways to do things better, more efficiently, more effectively.

Practical ideas - simply having ideas is not good enough. The ideas must be practical...can the ideas be put into daily practice?

A willingness to take responsibility - accountability and the willingness to stand up when you have done something wrong is paramount in leadership.

A completion factor – Leaders must be able to lead the people through the entire process. Followers may not follow the next time if the leader did not meet the goals from before.

Mental toughness – Leaders do not spend a lot of time worrying about what the people are saying. Leaders have their own internal mind-set that propels them forward to success even when others may think you need to "throw in the towel."

Peer respect- respect and being liked are not the same. Leaders are not necessarily overly-concerned about being liked. Leaders want to be respected for what they do and what they stand for.

Family respect – one of the best ways to judge a leader's character is to look at their family members and the level of respect they give to the individual. If the person's family does not show them respect, you should be concerned. Their true character is known to the family.

People listen to them – a leader does not waste a lot of time talking. Time is too important and so are words. Therefore, when most leaders speak, people listen to what they have to say. Leaders choose their words carefully and each word has meaning.

But even according to Smith, having these ten traits or qualities is simply not enough. The potential leader must have *character*. (Smith, p4) The only way to determine an individual's character is to *test* the individual in the environment in which they will be operating. Over time, their *true character* will come out. In addition, for a true leader exemplifying the behaviors previously identified, their *character* will be continually changing as they go through each new experience.

For Reflection...
> *"Every great journey takes place outside the comfort zone—no great journey is taken in solitude."*
> —Dr. Fred Finks

Integrity is the character quality of a leader that, over time, fosters genuine trust in leaders. Bill Perkins describes integrity and shares a story of testing.

INTEGRITY . . . THE HALLMARK OF CHARACTER
Bill Perkins[1]
Founder and president of the Million Mighty Men, author of
Awaken the Leader Within contributor to the *Leadership Bible*

It was a simple question and I expected a quick answer. As the CEO of the company that built Seattle's Space Needle, I knew Brad was quick on his feet.

---

[1] This article was adapted from chapter two of *Awaken the Leader Within* by Bill Perkins; Zondervan Publishing House, 2000.

But when I asked the question he paused, tilted his head to one side, placed his hand on his chin and contemplated an answer.

"Leaders of integrity?" he said out loud.

Finally he looked me in the eyes and said, "I know a man who has integrity in every area of his life." And then Brad hesitated as something came to his mind. "Well, there is one area where he lacks integrity—he's political and tells people what they want to hear in order to keep his options open."

He paused again and said, "And then there's a man I know who lives in New York. He has integrity in business—always keeps his promises. Once more he paused and then whispered, "He cheats on his wife though."

"Bill, I don't think I know a leader who possesses integrity in *every* area of his life. At least not once I get to know them."

Before he could continue his thought I interrupted. "What about you. You've got integrity, haven't you?

Brad lifted an eyebrow and said, "Yes, except in one area."

"What's that?"

"I care for people, but I have a hot temper."

My conversation with Brad took place a few hours ago and I'm still struggling with the implication of his words—"I don't know a leader who possesses integrity in *every* area of his life."

Are there no leaders of integrity among us? Is integrity, like a rainbow, something we can chase but never catch? Or, is our understanding of integrity so limited we don't understand exactly what it is and how to acquire it?

These are important questions because the people you lead want you to possess integrity. In fact, after researchers James Kouzes and Barry Posner surveyed thousands of people and performed more than four hundred written case studies they discovered people value honesty and integrity in a leader more than anything else. Virtually every person they talked with placed integrity on the top of their leadership wish list.[2]

Integrity is the foundation upon which the character of a leader will stand or fall. Whether you're leading a company, a church, a family, a battalion or an athletic team—those you lead want to know they can trust you. They want to follow you without fear of disappointment.

Integrity Defined

A biblical author once wrote, "Jesus Christ is the same yesterday and today and forever" (Hebrews 13:8). Jesus is both eternal and unchanging. If the author of Hebrews had wanted to use one word to describe Jesus as unchanging he could have said, "Jesus possesses *integrity*." The word *integrity* speaks of someone who is "whole or complete" and has the same root word as does the word *integrated* [3] A leader of integrity has taken the principals that govern his life (like the Ten Commandments), internalized them and integrated them into every area of his life.

A leader of integrity isn't like a weathervane that changes direction with every shift of the social winds. He's like a compass that is internally magnetized so it always points north regardless of what's happening around it. He is honest at work *and* at home. He keeps promises *even* if it means a financial loss. He speaks well of his clients in their presence *and* behind their back. He doesn't treat his wife with respect in public and belittle her behind closed doors. A leader of integrity doesn't switch masks to win the favor of the audience he's playing for.

Because leaders of integrity don't pretend to be something they're not, with them, what you see is what you get, literally. And it's not that leaders of integrity are perfect—they aren't. But they're aware of their weaknesses and don't lead others to believe they have no personal flaws. When my friend Brad admitted he cared for people but had a hot temper, while he didn't realize it, his statement demonstrated integrity.

---

[2] (Kouzes, James M., and Posner, Barry Z., *Credibility; How leaders gain and lost it, why people demand it.* San Francisco: Jossey-Bass, 1993, p. 14).
[3] (Random House Webster's college dictionary—2nd. Ed, Random House, Inc., 201 East 50th Street, New York, NY, 10022, 1997, p. 679).

As we finished lunch, Brad said, "You know Bill, only one man possessed perfect integrity." Of course, he's right. And if we're going to lead effectively we need to let the example of Jesus show us what integrity looks like and how it's cultivated.

A Closer Look

Nobody who endured the Watergate hearings will forget listening to the recorded conversations between President Richard Nixon and his closet advisers. Behind closed doors the President spewed forth obscenities like a seasoned sailor. The more we listened the more we realized Nixon's public and private persona were radically different.

Of course, Nixon isn't alone. In an effort to keep his "private" life "private" President Clinton repeatedly lied about his relationship with Monica Lewinsky. "Who wouldn't lie about an affair?" one news commentator asked, implying we should not only accept such lying but expect it from a leader under such circumstances.

The unending stream of scandalous information about national leaders has become so routine: many are insisting we view the private life of a leader as "off limits." Some insist, "As long as he gets the job done, it doesn't matter what he does in private."

Jesus didn't buy that philosophy. One day while walking along the shore of the Sea of Galilee he saw two fishermen mending their nets. He waved an arm and told the men to follow him. Immediately, Peter and Andrew left their nets, their boats and their fishing business and followed Jesus (Matthew 4:19-20). For the next three-and-a-half years they were as close to Jesus as his shadow. The man who led them pulled back the blinds of his private life and invited them look inside.

An Integrated Ethic

Because leaders of integrity consistently live out their ethic they aren't afraid of scrutiny. In 1836 Abraham Lincoln was campaigning for election to the Legislature when his opponent, Robert Allen, publicly claimed he possessed evidence of corruption that would destroy Lincoln's credibility. Allen promised to keep the details confidential as a favor to Lincoln. Of course, the mere mention of impropriety had the potential to so soil Lincoln's reputation he would lose the election.

Instead of wiping his brow and sighing in relief because Allen would keep the details to himself, Lincoln sent a letter to Allen with this exhortation: "That I once had the confidence of the people of Sangamon, is sufficiently evident, and if I have since done anything, either by design or misadventure, which if known would subject me to a forfeiture of that confidence, he that knows of that thing, and conceals it, is a traitor to his country's interest."[4]

As a leader of integrity Lincoln wasn't afraid of exposure—in fact, he insisted Allen bring forth every dirty fact regardless of the consequences he would suffer. Lincoln didn't fear exposure because there was nothing to expose.

One thing about Jesus that repeatedly frustrated his enemies was their inability to catch him doing something wrong. While he often disregarded their customs and ignored their prejudices, they never saw him lie or cheat. He consistently practiced the highest standard of ethics. He once said, "Do not think that I have come to abolish the Law or the Prophets; I have not come to abolish them but to fulfill them" (Matthew 5:17). Jesus could look at the entire moral code of the Old Testament, including the Ten Commandments, and say, "Those are the ethics I hold to and throughout the course of my life I have kept them perfectly." On one occasion he asked his enemies, "Can any of you prove me guilty of sin?" (John 8:46). And while their most brilliant legal experts followed Jesus around looking for some infraction of the law, they never found one.

If you want to be a leader of integrity you need to integrate your ethics into *every* area of your life. You don't want to be like the church leader who told me he practiced the "100 Mile Rule." When I asked him to explain the rule he said, "When I'm in town I conform to the rules of the church. But when I'm 100 miles away I can do whatever I want." Ultimately, his double life was uncovered and his nationally acclaimed ministry fell like a wounded bird.

Because leaders of integrity integrate their ethics into every area of their lives they possess a second characteristic—one a high school coach from Massachusetts desperately needed.

---

[4] (*The Life and Writings of Abraham Lincoln*) Philip Van Doren Stern, Random House, Inc., 1999, p. 226).

Authenticity

For over twenty years William "Nick Eddy" McMullen served as an assistant coach at Old Colony High School in New Bedford, Massachusetts. The head coach and student athletes were thrilled to have him coach at Old Colony. After all, Eddy was a former Notre Dame running back, a Heisman trophy finalist in 1966 who went on to play for the Detroit Lions.

For twenty years nobody knew the truth about McMullen—he was an imposter. His ruse would have continued if he hadn't agreed to meet with a fan of the real Eddy—a man who had met the football star while he played for Notre Dame. One look and the fan realized McMullen was a pretender. The real Eddy is 6-2 and weighs 200 pounds-plus, while the imposter stands 5-7 and weighs 160 pounds.

The fan telephoned the real Eddy who called McMullen and urged him to come clean. "I told him he could stop looking over his shoulder, waiting for the phone to ring."[5]

While few leaders would assume the name and history of another person, we all give false impressions. In an effort to strengthen our credibility we communicate an exaggerated level of honesty, care, commitment and knowledge. We pretend our strained marriages are healthy and our appetites are under control. How often has a CEO or head coach promised to remain with a company or team only to abandon ship for a higher paying more prestigious job? How often have political leaders made promises no man or woman could deliver? How often has a religious leader condemned the sins of others and later been caught committing the same sins?

Because leaders of integrity have integrated their ethics into every area of their life they communicate authentically with those they lead. They don't pretend to be someone they aren't. Because they speak openly about their strengths and weaknesses people trust them.

Toward the end of his life Jesus told his disciples, "Anyone who has seen me has seen the Father" (John 14:9). In essence he said, "When you look at me you're looking at God."

---

[5] (USA Today, Fri., Oct 8, 1999, page 7C, "Real Nick Eddy forgives fake one, Carolyn White).

41

His claim would have been ludicrous except for the fact that everything he ever said and did substantiated his statement. That's why Peter could confidently identify him as the Messiah, the Son of the living God (Matthew 16:16).

But remember, Jesus not only identified himself as the Son of God, but as the Son of Man. Peter not only saw Jesus walk on water, he saw him weep at the grave of Lazarus and heard him cry in Gethsemane. Jesus was authentic about his divinity *and* humanity. He allowed his disciples to see him as God and man.

If I'm going to lead with integrity not only will I consistently practice my ethics in every area of my life, I'll be honest about who I am. When I interviewed for my second pastorate I told the church, "I'll consistently provide you biblical messages that are insightful, entertaining and practical. I'll challenge the men to a deeper devotion to God and help the church grow."

Those are the sorts of things churches like to hear. But I also said, "I'm not detail oriented and my pastoral gifts of counseling and comforting aren't very strong." I made it clear if they were looking for a man who would hand out warm-fuzzes, they needed to keep looking.

I don't like pointing out my weaknesses to others. But because I'm committed to authenticity I refuse to pretend I'm someone I'm not. I want those I lead to know I'm the same on the inside as I appear on the outside. I'm sure you want that too. But if you know yourself well, you realize you're skilled at hiding what's on the inside. You've got a closet full of masks you can put on so you'll look better than you are. We all do.

While most of realize we hide behind masks it's especially painful when we're faced with the choice of continuing to hide or letting others see the truth. A number of years ago I realized I had lied to a team of people I led. At the time I convinced myself it wasn't a lie at all—just a convenient omission. As I reflected on what I had done it was especially painful because I thought lying was a problem *other* leaders had. I feared confessing my misdeed because doing so might sacrifice the trust and loyalty of my team.

On the outside I looked spiritual and courageous but on the inside I was scrambling to justify what I had done. I had a hard time accepting the fact that I, an honest man, had lied. More than anything I wanted to pretend I *never* exaggerated or distorted the truth for my

42

advantage. I wanted to be seen as a *perfect* leader deserving the unquestioning devotion of my followers. The question I asked myself was this: *What would a leader of integrity do when he realized he had lied?* It took every ounce of resolve I possessed to peel back the mask and reveal the ugly man hiding behind it. I found it easier to talk about the value of authenticity than to practice it—especially when doing so meant revealing a personal flaw.

As leaders it's easy to believe those under our charge are better off with the illusion of perfection than the truth about us. When I was in high school the father of one of my best friends was Cactus Pryor, a well-known television personality in Central Texas. His youthful face, thick brown hair and warm smile made Cactus one of the most recognized and loved men in Austin. I'll never forget the first time I saw him off-camera in the safety of his home—Cactus had no hair.

Like Cactus Pryor leaders often pretend to be something they're not. Nobody cares if a television personality wears a hairpiece, but it's different when a leader pretends to be something he or she isn't. Eventually those internal flaws will surface, like dandelion seeds in grass, and when they do inauthentic leaders will clamber to cover the flaws or discredit the person who pointed them out.

The Cultivation of Integrity

I mention our tendency to hide because I believe it's the greatest enemy we face in the development of integrity. Fear is a word that was never used in reference to Jesus. He never feared one of his disciples would see his humanity and believe he couldn't possibly be God and man.

Our problem is we know a gap exists between our ethics and our behavior. Nobody, except Jesus, was a moral ten. And that's the rub; we feel we should be a ten and want to give that impression.

I chuckle every time I think of the story in which a man died and stood at the gate of heaven. As he waited to get in an angel handed him a 100-pound stick of chalk and told him to climb a ladder that ascended into space and mark a rung for each sin he had committed during his life. After he had been climbing for several months and the piece of chalk was a tiny sliver he cried out in pain when somebody stepped on his hand. He looked up and saw Mother Theresa.

43

"What are you doing?" he yelled.

"I'm going down for more chalk," she replied.

I like that story because it illustrates the fact that even the most revered and seemingly holy leader does not perfectly measure up to Jesus. And as leaders we fear losing our influence if we allow those under our charge to see our flaws.

The men Jesus trained to lead his cause were no different than you and me. They held to a high moral ethic that they repeatedly violated and they were often out of touch with their personal shortcomings. They too tried to hide their weaknesses behind a mask and frequently denied they even existed.

Fortify Your Weaknesses

Of course, it's one thing to admit our tendency to hide behind a mask and another thing to throw it away. Unfortunately, many leaders will violate their ethic if the price is high enough. We can strengthen our integrity by admitting we overestimate how faithfully we practice it. I believe identifying gaps between our ethic and behavior is crucial if we're going to become leaders of integrity. To put it differently: We must know our weaknesses and fortify them.

Would You Violate Your Ethic?

You may have found that last paragraph a bit troubling. "I would never compromise my ethic," you may say. Really? Perhaps you need to reconsider. On the night before Jesus' crucifixion the Lord told Peter he would deny him three times. Peter said, "Even if I have to die with you, I will never disown you" (Matthew 26:35).
Peter professed the highest of all human ethics. He said he would die for Jesus. A few hours later, he did exactly as Jesus predicted. With each denial Peter proved his behavior did not measure up to his ethic.

Jesus knew Peter would one day lead the church. But he also knew the fisherman would deny him. That knowledge did not undermine the Lord's confidence in Peter's leadership ability. Shortly before predicting the apostle's denial Jesus said, "When you have turned back, strengthen your brothers" (Luke 22:32).

44

Peter discovered on that dreadful night that he loved himself more than Jesus. He learned that he wasn't the man of integrity he believed himself to be. That painful reality drove Peter to despair. After reports of the resurrection he told the other disciples, "I'm going out to fish" (John 21:3).

Peter must have wondered how a man like himself, with so little integrity, could ever possibly be of service to the Lord. What he would soon discover is that Jesus is not looking for perfect leaders, but for men and women who hold to a high ethic and seek to flesh it out in their lives. He wants leaders who are so committed to integrity they allow others to bring it to their attention when they exaggerate, break a promise, over promise, or compromise the truth for personal advantage.

History tells us Peter went on to be one of the pillars of the early church. He wrote of humility, forgiveness, and personal holiness. He became a leader of integrity but he never became perfect—remember, that's a description reserved for Jesus. Even as the church grew and his leadership role expanded, Peter remained open to the rebuke of those who spotted an inconsistency in his life (Paul pointed out Peter's hypocrisy in Galatians 2:11-16).

In a similar way you need to ask God, and a few trusted friends, to bring to your attention instances where you don't act with integrity. And as a leader you need to gently do the same thing for those you lead.

Avoid Hypocrisy

Several years ago I had a key leader tell me he felt I needed a softer touch in dealing with people. He said my abrasive style needed to be smoothed out some if I was going to be an effective leader.

Of course, he wasn't the first person to point out that flaw in my social style. Many others, including my wife, best friends, children, coaches, parents, neighbors, teammates, staff members, mailman, and others, had helped me realize I needed to be more sensitive when making a decision or pointing out a mistake in someone else.

The problem wasn't my lack of awareness in this area—I knew I needed to become more sensitive—it was that the man who confronted me had a bigger problem than my own. I had seen him verbally blast subordinates. On several occasions I had been the target of an outburst.

One day as we ate lunch alone in my office I asked him, "Dan, have you ever considered the possibility that one reason you're so troubled by my insensitivity is because it's a problem you struggle with."

He immediately became incensed. His face flushed. His muscles tightened. He locked his jaw, clinched his teeth and said, "I am not like you in this area." He was so offended by my suggestion that a short time later he left the team. The pain of facing his own sinfulness was so great he swept under the rug of consciousness all awareness of his own abrasive insensitivity.

He was a hypocrite in that area of his life. He held to a high ethic of sensitivity that he didn't practice. I saw the inconsistency so clearly I couldn't imagine how he missed seeing it himself. I suspect, as you read these words, you can call to mind numerous leaders you know who are just like that. Leaders who deny weaknesses in their character or personality style that are as visible to everyone around them as a mask.

Jesus' Harshest Words

If we're not open to correction then we run the risk of becoming inauthentic. The religious leaders of Jesus' day had developed an elaborate system of rituals (masks) that enabled them to appear better on the outside than they were on the inside. Over time they convinced themselves they were truly righteous people since they so diligently obeyed all of their man-made rules.

Jesus unleashed his harshest words on them because they professed a high ethic but didn't put it into practice. He told them, "You are like whitewashed tombs, which look beautiful on the outside but on the inside are full of dead men's bones and everything unclean. In the same way, on the outside you appear to people as righteous but on the inside you are full of hypocrisy and wickedness" (Matthew 23:27-28).

You've probably noticed that hypocrisy is one of those sins most of us can spot in others without seeing it in ourselves. It's like bad breath. If somebody else has it you want to keep your distance. But nobody can tell if their own breath is sweet or sour.

Look at Yourself

Now, go look in a mirror. As you gaze at your reflection, ask yourself, "Do I have weaknesses others can see that I refuse to face.

Weaknesses I pretend are absent or under control? Or, am I the kind of person who is comfortable with my strengths and weaknesses and allows others to see both?"

An Unexpected Test

It's a fact of life that you never know when your integrity will be tested. That's a lesson learned by am ambitious nurse who was being considered to lead the nursing team at a prestigious hospital. The chief of surgery had just completed an operation in which she was assisting when he snapped off his surgical gloves and told her to close the incision.

"But doctor, you've only removed eleven sponges. We used twelve."

"I removed them all," the doctor declared. "Now close the incision."

"No!" the nurse objected. "We used twelve sponges and there are only eleven on the table."

"I'll take full responsibility," the surgeon said sternly. "Suture."

"You can't do that," the nurse insisted. "What about the patient?"

The surgeon smiled, lifted his foot, and showed the nurse the twelfth sponge, which he had hidden under his shoe. Smiling, he said, "You'll do. The nursing team is yours to lead."

That nurse passed the integrity test. She held to the highest standard of patient care and put it into practice—even when a promotion was at stake.

Every day you'll face similar tests. They'll be unannounced. Some will be subtle and others will be in your face. Whether you know it or not those you lead will be watching you. They'll observe how you handle those unexpected character tests. As you allow the wisdom of Jesus to awaken the leader within you, your integrity will grow. As it does those you lead will trust you more. As their trust grows so will their eagerness to follow you.

Of course, integrity alone doesn't make an effective leader. Skilled leaders have to know were they're going. In the next chapter you'll discover how the wisdom of Jesus can enable you to become a visionary leader.

For Reflection...
  "In all of my actions, I am accountable and responsible to God."—Senator Bill Harris

A loss of integrity comes from an inward "disconnect" as

described by Paul Blease. He shares the conversations he has had with

some of the highest producers in the world of finance.

A LOSS OF INTEGRITY
Paul Blease
Director of Advanced Training at
Salomon Smith Barney in New York

I was asked to take over training all of our largest producers at Solomon-Smith-Barney. The person that asked me is Tom Matthews. He is an old style marine, "take the hill," kind of guy.

I said, to him, "Let me tell you what I wouldn't teach your best people. I won't teach them how to sell, market, attract assets or work with clients".

His reply was, "What are you going to teach them"?

Our best producers were hired to be high-end sophisticated sales people that can manage assets. They are entrepreneurial personalities, basically, John Wayne in a business suit. One day they wake up running a business with people, technology, and infrastructure. Name one John Wayne film in which he played an executive. That is the kind of person,

48

whether male or female that must now run a business. That's the first thing I teach them business structurally, systemically, technologically and interpersonally.

The second dynamic I address in our top producers is the type "A" personality I don't simply approve there overall productivity and effectiveness at work at the sacrifice of either their health, their personal life or their spiritual life. I have no interest in creating a productive human being that drops dead from a heart attack at 55 because the last time they went to a gym was in high school or they are on their third marriage because they do not go home. Or, has a spiritual crisis because, near the end of that life they realized they have climbed the ladder of success only to find out it is leaning against the wrong wall.

The third dynamic is perspective. In our industry, our top producers' sense of self-worth and value ebbs and flows with the markets. That is ridiculous. Think of designing anything around that construct in your life. Think about basing your marriage around something so arbitrary. You walk into your home and say, "Honey, I'm home!" Then, the plates come flying and you suspect that the market was down that day. That is not how you build a relationship or any sense of worth.

Those are the three things that I asked to do and to Tom's credit, he said, "I have no idea how you are going to do that. Frankly, I don't know much about what you just said. It sounds intriguing."

We had a 500-person seminar, 2 ½ days, with no agenda. The following week we received 375 emails that said things like, "Life-changing", "First time anyone spoke to me as a human being and not just a producer". It resonated throughout the firm. We were the "buzz" in the firm, for about three months. It gave us the latitude to take this whole thing forward. It has been the triad for the series that we have done for the last four years.

Confidence and Purpose

One of the things that we talk to our people about is the fusion of confidence and purpose. What we found is that when who you are fuses with what you do the power is immeasurable. How can you fuse what you do at Solomon-Smith Barney to create, not just an incredible business, but an incredible life.

In the film, "Chariots of Fire," Eric Little personifies the fusion of who he is with what he does. He is a Christian who based his life on the loftiest principles. But, he was also a great runner. And when you fuse those two, you find an incredible life. In Little, the way he ran personified his faith. Eric Little was the only runner in the history of sports that, when he hit full tilt as a sprinter, his head went completely back, almost an act of physical release. He never veered out of his lane. In the film clip, Eric states, "*I believe God made me for a purpose – He also made me fast and I am going to run with pleasure*". When you have a fusion of who you are with what you do you get that passion and you feel His pleasure. That is what you must uncover in what you do.

Volatile Personalities

If you have ever been around extraordinary achievers, there is an edge, volatility, intensity, sometimes it comes out as intensity, sometimes as volatility. When it gets pathological, I get involved. I have found that all of our top producers have a high level of confidence. Confidence is based on the task: I can do it! When you feel confident, you feel confident about your capacity to do something. It is a task orientation. However, there is another element that comes into play: Self-esteem. Self-esteem asks, "Am I worthy?" I have found that if there is a disconnect between confidence and self-esteem, volatility will emerge.

I work with people that have confidence bordering on arrogance coupled with low self-esteem. They can do the job, but they lack a sense of worthiness. This comes out in one-on-one conversations. It almost always stems from how they were raised. They are trying to prove someone wrong; oftentimes, fathers, sometimes other people.

One individual invited me to his home after a day of working with his management team. He indicated he had some individual issues that "I need to talk to you about". In the 5-hour conversation that followed, the disconnect between confidence in the job and personal work in the soul emerged. On one hand, there was this businessperson that was Machiavellian on the other side was this born-again Christian who had a wonderful family, wonderful church life and all the great stuff in life. This was a disconnect from his childhood, where he learned the classic, "I'll show you" type of behavior in response to a very autocratic, demanding father where nothing was ever good enough."

Everything in this man's life was designed to win favor, and, in our culture, you win favor through tangible accomplishments. This drives your confidence level very high but does nothing for your self-esteem. Self-esteem is, "Am I worthy in spite of…and without an reference to my performance." Brought up to be measured on his performance, he said that he had always been afraid that if he let down his guard, he would loose his edge and would cease to perform to his current level. He said, "This is what drives me."

I asked him if he understood that is not what drives him. What drives him is how he is wired, "You are a type 'A' personality. You will achieve at this point, based on habit, based on who you have become. Why you achieve will change if you bring this person that you are at home and in church into your business life. You'll still achieve, but the reason for the accomplishment will change. Rather than to prove your dad and everybody else wrong, it will be to fulfill and fuse who you are with what you do. Your mission will change. The 'why' will change. Your sense of fulfillment will dramatically improve. Your stress level will dramatically decrease. You live in a constant state of stress. Every time you fail to achieve marginally, your self-esteem is again hammered. It is a no-win scenario."

What you see in the volatility issue is a lack of maturity. A person will stop growing, emotionally, at some point in childhood. As an adult you put a façade over the child. You dress for success and you are more articulate. You have possessions. You look like an adult. But you are really a child saying, "I hope no one figures this thing out."

One of the problems is that when you have a high level of confidence, bordering on arrogance, people figure you can take it. They come at you head on. Then, you blow up. No one sees that low self-esteem beneath the façade unless they really know the person and they really love them.

The question I always get from people is, "How do I create high self esteem?" I cannot use the word "Christ" in a business setting so I use, "it's a spiritual element." It is a "spiritual connection." But, in this setting I have an audience that I can speak plain—it is called "grace." "Grace" says, "I love you, period!" That is the conversation I have with some of our largest producers in the Salomon, Smith, Barney organization.

Adversity and Principles

Make a list of character traits of the heroes that you admire. Where do you develop character, through adversity or ease? It is always adversity. It is character that comes out through conquering adversity that we admire. Character traits are based on universal principles. I use the word principle where others might use the phrase, "spiritual truth." Principles are universal truths that govern success and failure. They are impervious to your opinion. I like to deal in truth. You can trace virtually every time you have succeeded to adherence to one or more principles. And you can trace, virtually every failure you have experienced to the violation of one or more principles.

A starting list of principles includes: balance, discipline, and differed gratification.

Mission and Vision

Once you have the understanding of principles you can begin to build a mission and vision. The problem is if you don't have the right principles you can take you off in a direction you do not want to go.

Mission. Why are you in the boat? Why did you choose your profession? You could have chosen from thousands of professions – why this one and how does being here fulfill who you are and where you are trying to go? So why are you in the profession?

Vision. Where you are taking your profession. You can have people in the profession for the same reason going in very different directions. From that vision, you can then begin to build goals. As Steve Covey says, *"working with the end in mind."*

Mission must answer the question, "Why?" The purpose of a person or business that has no mission becomes, "Making Money." In lieu of a true mission that defines your soul the default is, "I get paid".

Vision is, "what is the one thing that you are here to do in your lifetime?" This actually came to me in a revelation sitting in a movie theatre. That vision has to be simple because through that vision you must filter everything that happens to you. If you think of the great people that we admire in history, their message and their vision was simple. Everything filtered through it. The one I point to is Lincoln, "preserve the Union". Everything filtered through that. For Ghandi, "independence". Everything filtered through that. You will be stretched through mission and vision.

Comfort Zone

If you are not stretched outside of your comfort zone on a regular basis, there is no growth. And there is no mission and vision that is stretching you to become what God gave you capability to become. My mission is to help everyone I come in contact with to become what God gave them the capacity to become. That filters everything that I do. The problem with the comfort zone is that it is either expanding, based on your actions or it is contracting. I worked in the retirement community as a broker early in my career. I saw this graphically; people whose comfort zones, whose worlds shrunk and shrunk over time. It never happened consciously; it happened because they were not pushing the envelope.

Perspective

The final thing I talk about is perspective. On your deathbed, when you look back on your life. Your definition of success may be slightly different. So, why not go there today and work backwards. Let's talk about what is going to be truly of value to you at that point in life and let's make sure we begin to build what you are going to value then, now. Because, as I have used the analogy before, "there is nothing worse in life than climbing the ladder of success only to find it is against the wrong wall at the time when it is too late to change." So, I say, "when you get home tonight for God sakes, go play catch with your kids, go to their games, take your wife on a date." That is what is important.

If you want to learn how to get people to trust you, begin by learning how you can trust God.

> *"Trust in the Lord with all your heart and lean*
> *not on your own understanding; in all your ways*
> *acknowledge him, and he will make your paths*
> *straight." Proverbs 3:5-6 (NIV)*

Learning Exercise #2:
Building a Foundation of Credibility

Read and discuss the Lovett Weems' article with a small group of three or four people. Then, as a group, design a plan for developing credibility in the first six months of a new leadership assignment. Develop a purpose statement, a series of objectives, and actionable goals.

Purpose:

Objectives:

Actionable Goals:

Learning Exercise #3:
Designing a Framework of Accountability

In a small group, read and discuss Valerie. Brown's article. Ask each person to share three ideas, arguments, or illustrations with which they identify.

1.

2.

3.

Continue the discussion by exploring the kinds of accountability systems and structures that would support you in your leadership assignment.

Learning Exercise #4:
Building the Walls of Integrity

In a small group, read and discuss the article by Bill Perkins. Share the part of the article that was most encouraging to you; share the part of the article that was most challenging to you.

Have you ever experienced (as a leader or as a follower) a breakdown of integrity? What were the results for you?

Can you remember a time when you experienced a triumph of integrity? What were the results for you?

Learning Exercise #5:
If You Climb the Walls, Climb the Right Walls

Read the article by Paul Blease and discuss it with a small group. Where did the article strike home for you?

To what degree do you believe *"my ladder is against the right wall"*?

Can you state the difference between your vision (what you're trying to do) and your mission (why you're trying to do it)?

Can you share a time when there was a "disconnect" between who you are and what you were doing as a leader?

Did you (and if so, how) experience the grace of Christ at that time?

Learning Exercise #6:
Making an Appraisal of My Leadership Character

The task of leadership has not changed. Leaders move and influence people to work together toward the accomplishment of mission. What has changed is the situation of leadership. The leaders power to move and influence others no longer rests primarily in a position of authority but in a relationship of trust.

Consider your personal response to the following questions:

• As the leader, how do I engender trusting relationships so that our organization can work together in healthy ways to accomplish our mission?

• As the leader, in what ways have I developed systems, structures, and support that protect and verify the trust that is placed upon me?

• When is the following statement is true: *The character pattern of integrity – speak the truth, keep your promise, and be authentic – will, over time and consistency, foster genuine trusting relationships*? Are there times when this statement doesn't apply?

• How do I become aware of my inward disconnects (brokenness) and turn to embrace the grace of Christ that makes me a whole person (heals me)?

Chapter 3
Leadership Character: Discovering Your Way

A leader's character is exposed in the level of the follower's trust. There are patterns of behaving and relating that create trust between a leader and followers. Leaders that are trusted are credible, accountable people of integrity. They are rooted in a personal vision with which followers can identify.

We now come to the question of how to develop personal leadership character. In this chapter, you will read the stories and reflections of six leaders on the journey of character development. The first thing you will notice is that each journey is unique, expressing the interplay between personality and leadership assignment.

- For a leader in the Justice Department, it is "the tip of the sword," but for the president of a Christian college it is "the mind of Christ...in the midst of conflict."
- For a young businesswoman, it is "perfect integrity" in every conversation. For a veteran pastor seeking to transition the church to a new leader, it is finding and supporting a successor.

- For a high school music teacher, it is a vision to "aim students in the right direction" in order to keep them growing. The leader of a nonprofit that helps hurting families considers "the right Mentor" as her key element in personal character development.

The journeys are unique, but there is a common framework.

First, each leader expresses *abiding passion*. It may be in a love for people, the vision of the institution, or to be a prize-winning organization. The passion is expressed in a sense of mission. This is more than what they do, it tells us why they do it.

Second, each leader has a *personal plan* for personal development. For some, it is laid out in clear steps. For others, it is seizing opportunities as they come. For some, it involves a larger dream that holds them to the path.

Third, each leader *needs people* in developing leadership character. Perhaps it is a formal arrangement with mentors. It might be a network of other professionals that give guidance and opportunities for reflection. For some, it is seeking out wise counsel and expert advice.

For Reflection…
> *"Being a leader of integrity demands that I lead from this place; this authentic reality of who I am and what God has called me to do."*—Jaime Gillespie

Story #1: Holding It Together

LeBron Fairbanks is President of Mt. Vernon Nazarene College. LeBron locates leadership in the midst of tensions, the irreconcilable differences, and conflicts that are part of every educational institution. Leadership development grows out of a personal and shared vision of servanthood. He views leadership development as a relational exchange between the leader and those being led. As they come to a shared identity, a shared calling, and a shared understanding of how they will "live together as the family of God," deep character is developed. He delineates five characteristics of the servant leader. It is these characteristics that can transform the tension implicit in the organization into the energy needed to move forward.

For Reflection...
> *"At the core of a leader must be the desire*
> *to serve rather than be served."* —Mary Kaufmann

"PERSONAL LEADERSHIP CHARACTER FORMATION"
E. LeBron Fairbanks
President, Mt. Vernon Nazarene College

If "in Christ all things are made new" then how does our relationship with Christ convert our leadership lifestyle? The question pursues a spirituality of leadership.

Where does Christian spirituality and spiritual leadership intersect in the context of a Christian community? In the midst of conflicting expectations, and often irreconcilable differences, the Christian leader is a local congregation, mission organization, Christian

61

college, a church governing board, or a host of other communities, what does it mean—really mean—in these often conflicting situations to lead with the mind of Christ?

I am often challenged by the words of "The Servant Song" in our hymnal (page 679). Listen to the first two verses:

> *Brother, let me be your servant,*
> *Let me be as Christ to you;*
> *Pray that I may have the grace*
> *To let you be my servant too.*
>
> *We are pilgrims on a journey;*
> *We are brothers on the road,*
> *We are here to help each other,*
> *Walk the mile and bear the load*

Each time I sing this hymn, however, I am haunted by a question. Is it really possible to be a servant—a servant leader—in the real world of the contemporary Christian community with all of the conflicting demands and pressures placed on us?

My contention is that, regardless of where God places us as leaders and with whom He places us within the Christian fellowship, we need—we must have at the core of our being—at least three compelling convictions:

- A vision of who we are as people of God;
- A passion for what we are called to do in the work of God; and
- An obsession for how we live together as the family of God.

These convictions are the heart and soul of the servant leadership. They comprise the essence of the Servant's Song.
I am coming to understand that if leaders are to assist "the led" to think and act Christianly, we must wholeheartedly embrace these leadership themes:

- The motivation for servant leadership is grounded in a theology of ministry.
- The lifestyle of servant leadership is characterized by a passion for Christ-likeness.
- The goal of servant leadership is for transformation and reconciliation.

62

- The ministry of servant leadership is to prepare others for their ministries.
- The evidence of servant leadership is in the qualitative growth of the led—individually and collectively.

My thesis is that there must be a vision within the Christian community we serve regarding ministry that is shared by both the leader and the led. Without this shared vision of ministry, the community of faith will experience disintegration and despair. Conversely, mobilizing a Christian community for ministry hinges on a radical commitment to our identity as:

- brothers and sisters in Christ,
- fellow travelers on a spiritual journey
- members together of Christ's body,
- a fellowship of God's people,
- a microcosm of the kingdom of God on earth,
- a community of faith,
- a sacramental community in and through which the grace of God flows.

Fundamentally, I believe, effective leadership for character formation ministry expression is grounded in biblical perspective and not in organizational skills. Skills, of course, are needed. However, sharp skills without Christian motives easily lead to manipulation. The primary orientation and motivation of our actions as Christian leaders must be deeply theological. Brother, sister, let me be your servant...

Story #2: Being On Point

Marc Farmer is the Chief Inspector of Judicial Protective Services for the United States Marshals Service. This is an organization of more than 4,000 officers nationwide. Marc also has more than 22 years of ministry experience in the local church. For Marc, leadership is located in the crisis, when "the wagons are circled." A person must accept the leadership role. Some leaders are passive, only exhibiting leadership qualities when the situation demands. Other leaders are directive in developing their leadership potential and character. A directive leader comes to grips with the way her or his life has been "encoded" by upbringing, circumstance, and experience. But, a directive leader also makes decisions in how to "decode" their life-learning into leadership decisions. Character is seen in the way you "decode." Good character is based on an internal framework that is at the same time consistent and dynamic.

For Reflection...
> *"Character is revealed in the face of*
> *adversity—courage is action in spite of fear."*
> —Bev Spreng

PERSONAL LEADERSHIP CHARACTER DEVELOPMENT
Marc Farmer
Chief Inspector, Judicial Protective Services
United States Marshals Service

A leader is someone others will follow. Leadership is not a special set of qualities for the moment. A leader gains the trust of followers. The desire of followers is to know which way is out. A leader is seen as a source of support and strength, one who gives direction, especially when the "wagons are circled". Leaders possess a set of dominant traits which are consistently manifested in almost an unconscious manner – they do not have to think to be—they are...and followers seem to know intuitively who they are—we follow them. Yet these traits can be sharpened, but under one condition, personal acceptance.

Personal leadership development does not begin until one acknowledges and accepts that she or he is a leader. Not until one understands they are "called" to be the "tip of the sword." In many instances, it is the initial point of impact. Consequently, a sword tip must be sharpened, polished, used, evaluated for its characteristics and retooled to produce its best capabilities. Leadership character development is the process of intentional actions by a person who has actively accepted a call of leadership. No one can be a leader without some degree of personal acceptance coupled with a manifest desire to be a leader, to take the lead.

There are active-passive leaders, those who possess a certain set of traits and a sense of situational direction. People follow them. This type of leader is driven by circumstance, and is reluctant to work on self-development. They are active-passive because they will only maneuver the sword of leadership momentarily; this is situational leadership.

There are also active-directive leaders. They are the ones who accept the role and responsibility of leadership. It is at this point when one realizes their personal desire to enter into consciously a process leadership development.

And yet, leadership development is preceded by leadership formation; the foundational stage of becoming a leader is related to one's gestalt; one's perception of things happening in the world. It has to do with the role one plays out in their world-context, and the role one chooses to play. Each person is born into a world in which they are encoded with a system of values, culture norms, family beliefs and personal beliefs. Each person is encoded with an internal life matrix something within from which something else originates or develops. Accordingly, one's life matrix has a direct influence on *how* and *what* choice one makes.

Let's look at the how and what of leadership formation, noting that absent the ability to analyze a particular leader's life, it would be reasonably fair to conclude that every leader has been encoded from the day of their birth. The process of encoding in not an end-all process, it is only one side of the leadership formation process. Decoding is equally a part of a leader's life. Both, encoding and decoding are a process of figuring out what is good or bad, right or wrong. It is employing one' life-matrix as an internal decision table, which in some instances sets the stage for courses of action chosen by a leader. It is the ongoing process of encoding and decoding that ultimately defines a leader and the method employed by a leader in making leadership decisions.

Up to now, one may conclude that this reflection is just a two-prong approach to thinking about personal leadership character

65

development, e.g., encoding and decoding, good or bad, or the how and what of leadership. Well, the head has two eyes, it has two ears, and the nose has two nostrils, they are only information-ports. The human mind can divide and evaluate the information received in hundreds of ways, proving for us hundreds of new ways to consider the topic of leadership.

Having touched on half of the theme of "Personal Leadership Character Development," let's take a glimpse at character development in the context of leadership. Character development is a result of the encoding and decoding process which formulates a life-matrix, from the 'how' we make decisions, and the 'why' people follow. Character development involves acts of internal prioritization. It is the result of reconciling conflicting values and issues of culture. Character has to do with personal ownership of guiding principals that have been etched into a leader's heart, mind and soul. Character is more than preference or style; it is the line of demarcation. It is the most consistent element in the life of a leader. It is character that gains the trust of those who follow. Character is not static; iIt is a framework of internal reference. This idea of a framework is captured in words of the Psalmist David who said, "I have hidden your work in my heart that I might not sin against you."

Story #3: To Help Somebody

Larita Hand is the founder and executive director of Mercy Missions, a nonprofit organization that ministers to the broken-hearted and families in crisis and provides training for short-term missions through pastoral counseling, mentoring, discipleship, spiritual retreats, and conferences. For Larita, the task of leadership is to help others identify and build their own strengths and abilities. Leadership development is expressed in a commitment to a plan (study, discipleship, moral and ethical behavior), but results in deep character traits (integrity, honesty, trustworthiness, and excellence). Character development involves a relationship with a mentor and using the opportunities in your current leadership challenge.

For Reflection...
> *"True leadership is about being honest with yourself through self assessment and accountability groups."*—Valerie K. Brown

Personal Leadership Development
Larita Hand
Executive Director, Mercy Missions

The greatest challenge to good leadership for me is the commitment to give excellent service to those I am serving. I believe that the good leader should empower others in leadership and help them identify their own abilities and strengths in Leadership Character development through this empowerment the leader is constantly evaluating their own challenges to excellence.

The call to the Gospel ministry required a commitment to study, discipline, morality and ethical behavior. However, in my seminary years I began to develop the leadership characteristics of integrity, humility, trustworthiness and excellence.

In my lifetime I have had the experience of mentoring others but it was through the process of being mentored that I began to experience the changes in my personal development of leadership character. The mentor talked with me about my weakness and strengths. The mentor then challenged me to conquer my fears through putting me in leadership roles that required me to conquer my fears and promoted leadership character.

67

The key leadership issue that I am dealing with now is Integrity in Decision Making. The Nonprofit Organization Leader is constantly making changes to adapt to the changes in the community, society, politics in government and bequest of executive board members within the organization. I am the visionary in the organization. I share the vision with the board and they make decisions based on my dreams for the organization. I am presently challenged with making the moral and ethical decisions for the fundraising methods.

I have determined to do the following; First, to re-examine my own personal core values regarding my development of integrity in ministry; Secondly, to re-examine the core values of the nonprofit organization and reconstruct new ideas about the integrity of the organization; Thirdly, to obtain professional advice from lawyers, tax consultants and foundation organizations about the ethical implications of certain types of fundraisers; Fourthly, to create a realistic fundraiser plan and present it to the executive board and my plans for execution of the plan; Fifthly, to avoid making financial decisions based on deficits and losses.

For Reflection...
> *"If one is to be effective, the effort to lead with honesty is the overwhelming stamp of approval needed. Honesty is the revealing quality of authenticity."*—Rod Bushey

Story #4: In the Stress of the Moment

Mary Kaufmann is the Director of Sales Development for the Longaberger Company. Her responsibilities include helping develop and implement company initiatives that will strengthen relationships with sales associates and customers. For Mary, leadership character is at stake in every conversation. To be "perfect" in integrity demands a sense of wholeness, consistency, and maturity that is measured in the person who is willing and able to tell the truth and keep promises. The

challenge and opportunity for leaders is when integrity is uncomfortable.

A variety of strategies and skills is helpful when they are under girded

with a deep passion and longing. For Mary, integrity is finding ways to

make the living presence of Jesus Christ clear in each situation.

For Reflection...
> *"To lead in times of profound change*
> *demands both courage and character, and I must be*
> *the change I seek to produce in others. As I continue*
> *to work through this relationship, I will probably*
> *experience, increasingly, the "pain of leadership."*
> *The "character" issue is not just a component of*
> *leadership formation, it is the core."*
> —E. LeBron Fairbanks

LEADING AT EVERY MOMENT
Mary Kaufmann
Director, Sales Development
Longaberger Company

The greatest challenge of good leadership for me is to act with "perfect" integrity in every casual conversation. I am in hundreds of conversations every day where I am presented with many opportunities to act with or without integrity. In these conversations character issues surface in the form of inappropriate jokes and stories, foul language and gossip introduced by others.

Like the adage " you never know what's inside a cup until it's bumped," it is no secret that one's true character is reflected during times of great stress. These times of stress may occur at rare and random intervals. I dare to say our character is more accurately revealed during those many hours in a day while we are in conversation. It is these "moment by moment" instances that, in totality, reflect what is inside us and who we really are.

Time spent in church and with my family causes little friction. Clearly I'm able to interact with ease during these situations reflecting the character by which I strive to live. My greater challenge is when with people outside my comfortable circle. Using silence, showing little interest, or changing the subject are tactics I use when inappropriate issues surface in conversation. Even so, these skills need to be sharpened.

The key leadership character issue I am dealing with right now relates to how I spend my time at work. Over the years I have developed a network of people who come to me for information and guidance.

During the past several years, the scope of my responsibilities has broadened. I now am leading projects and a team of people. In the past, my door has always been open, but today, in order to meet my new work demands, I am not as accessible as I would like to be to other employees with personal struggles. My challenge is maintaining the delicate balance between the demands of my position and my desire to serve others.

Several months ago I began sharing the healing power of Jesus more freely with my co-workers. When people come to me with a problem, if I see a window for sharing the gospel, I suggest prayer as an answer. I am turning this challenge into an opportunity to facilitate the development of faith and ultimately hope and peace in the lives of others. I am creating positive change by setting a caring standard of servant leadership for others to follow.

My goal for personal leadership is to bring Christian integrity to areas where I see a crisis of leadership. I hope through strengthening my own character I will bring stronger moral character both to those I lead, and to those who lead others.

For Reflection…
> *"My character has to be the foundation of my professional accomplishments for these accomplishments to be personally meaningful."*—Kush Pittenger

Story #5: Grace in Transition

Charles Lake is the founding pastor of Greenwood Community Church, Greenwood, Indiana. For Charles, leadership is in the transition. Transition has an external and an internal component. Leaders know that it is not enough to set a date, determine a strategy, and implement tactics in order to see an organization through change. There is a change in identity, in attitude, and in organizational culture. In this brief article, Charles reminds us that this same pattern is true in the heart of the leader. It is one thing to set a plan for transitioning the church to new leadership. It is another to develop the character qualities needed to support the transition as the outgoing leader.

Personal Leadership Character Formation
Rev. Charles Lake
Founding Pastor, Greenwood Community Church

Centers for Leadership Development were not know at seminaries when I attended. The word "mentoring" was not a part of the theological language spoken. Leadership was not a common trait in the family of my upbringing and I can't recall anyone ever telling me that leadership character is indeed unique to character in general. In looking back, I suppose experience has been my best teacher but by no means the easiest or most painless.

In later years, the studies connected with the pursuit of my doctorate, a wave of new literature on the subject and the increased emphasis on mentoring have challenged me to explore the subject further, not only as a subject to be studied by a lifestyle to pursue. My love for the reading of biographies of great leaders has always been a

71

consistent contributor to my understanding of character qualities needed in an effective leader.

At his juncture in my life and ministry, I feel confronted with character issues relating to the eventual transitioning of leadership from a founder-leader to a new and more contemporary leader who will carry on the vision earlier imparted. Such transitions in the church of Jesus Christ have a greater failure rate than a successful one. It is very important to me to make a success of this inevitable challenge.

During the days of my seminary training in the early '60's, I witnessed a transfer of leadership in the position of our seminary president. A president of over 20 years, chose and mentored his own successor with the approval of the Seminary Board of Trustees. The "transition of power" went remarkably smooth and the institution was strengthened as a result of the transition. My observations have led me to believe that the success of the transition was largely due to the character of the predecessor as a leader. No single trait stood out, but rather a combination of character traits that made an indelible impression on me.

First, the ability of the predecessor to see in his successor the gifts and attributes necessary to function efficiently and effectively in the position. The years that followed validated the choice. The new leader took the seminary to stages of development never before dreamed.

The care of the predecessor in accepting and applauding the successes of the young successor also demonstrated strong leadership character. The seminary constituency shares the joy of the preceding president in each and every accomplishment of his mentoree. His constant support and public affirmation of the new president were frequently heard and always received as authentic and genuine. The ability to rejoice in the successes of others is without question a strong leadership character trait.

As that day of challenge approaches for me, I am seeking to prepare myself without waiting to the last minute. I have already interviewed some leaders who have been through that experience. Although there is little in print covering the topic, I have sought to read as extensively as possible while sharing my findings with those who are in authority over me. I am seeking to work in tandem with our Board of Elders to facilitate a transition that is acceptable to them and that is in the best interests of the congregation. I look forward to the opportunity to prove leadership character in this significant transition both in my life, the life of my family and the church congregation.

For Reflection...
> *"To be an effective leader I need to be an effective person of credibility and unconditional love."*
> — Jonathan Dowdy

Story #6: Everyone is Watching

Rod Bushey has been a high school choral director for almost thirty years, leading award-winning choirs and developing exceptional musicians. He shares the story of his personal development as a leader. His story demonstrates the truth: Leadership is something you learn on the job, and you learn it while everyone is watching you. Rod approached leadership with a "jump in and make it happen" attitude. He looked for help in every direction. He was searching for the guiding principle and vision of his own spirit, and came to a few clear principles that guide him. He models these principles in his own life.

AIM THEM IN THE RIGHT DIRECTION
Rod Bushey
High School Choral Director
Howell, Michigan

Majoring in music was not exactly a dream when I went to college. Although music was a major part of my life, my interests were broader than that subject. I thought teaching would be in my future, but my concentration was in the area of instrumental music, not choral music for which I have made my living for the past thirty years. My hope was to minor in physical education while majoring in music. The college did not offer a curriculum for such a diverse area of study. That plunged me headfirst into a program of music education.

After searching and interviewing for "band" positions to no avail, I was offered the choir position at Howell High School in August of 1972. The first day, the choir sang a selection that they claimed "...was ready to sing, we all know it". I was ready to resign after the first hearing. Perhaps it was a diamond in the rough but I was not able to recognize anything resembling a diamond that first day.

The dream of a great choir program was not born that first year. The major focus was to formulate a plan to begin to generate interest and build a foundation for good music education program.

Realizing my strengths and incorporating those into a teaching style was one of the challenges. There were also a number of resources tapped to help me improve my understanding of this new profession. My main help came from other directors who ran successful programs. From their selection of music, approach to choral tone, to activities that had proven effective, I gleaned as much information as possible.

Enthusiasm and transparency have been two factors that have helped me work with high school and middle school students. My attitude of perseverance, regardless of the circumstances, helped keep the kids believing. In my second year, the first year of my large, auditioned choir, I decided to take the choir to festival. The Monday prior to Saturday's choral festival, my father went in for surgery and I felt it necessary to be there. The kids were anxious about me being gone but assured me they would continue concentrated rehearsals.

When I returned the next day, they were very pleased with themselves for working out some details in the music to help prepare them for the weekend performance. Their work paid off and we received our first superior rating. As we continued to improve as a choir, the department gained in numbers along with the quality of performances.

There were a number of statements made to me before and during my early years that influenced and motivated me greatly. One such statement was: "just aim high school kids in the right direction, and get out of the way".

Those words instilled a motivation in me along with the fear of not being certain how to aim". However, I learned to trust my instinct and communicate directly with the students. One characteristic of good leadership is to recognize your strengths and work to overcome your weakness. It has been apparent to me, and pointed out by several colleagues and friends, that I have a gift to communicate with young people. That personality trait originates from having a "heart for kids" and has punctuated my career in education.

During my first year of teaching, a junior named Carol was a member of my choir. She was seated next to David, the son of a pastor in our town, in whose church I was the minister of music. Carol began dating David, attending the church, and joined the church. I made an extra effort to encourage her and let her know how important she was to the success of the high school choir. At the end of her junior year, she auditioned for and was selected as member of the select chamber choir. Little did I know, Carol was considering quitting school halfway through the eleventh grade. In June, I received a note from her parents. A portion of it read: "Thank you for encouraging Carol this year. If it were not for the choir program, she would have quit school. You were the primary influence that kept her in school".

As a young teacher, that note alone helped validate my first year in education. By the way, Carol attended a Christian university, married David, is the mother of three children, and became successful in the banking industry. For example, a good family friend brought her fifteen-year old nephew to the lake one week in the summer, a number of years ago. He was quite far from home and had no acquaintances in the area. I met him at the end of the dock one morning and we began talking. I asked a few questions, we chatted a bit longer and before long, he spent the remained of the day together. His aunt commented on how easily he warmed up to me. She said he had not spoken with anyone for a few days and was pleased that he and I connected so quickly.

It seems safe to say that successful leadership comes from having a heart for those you serve. Without that distinction, I would have left the field of education years ago. There is an energy surrounding young people reminding me of my own youth. Often times I find I live vicariously through my own students. That may sound strange, but I was somewhat insecure as a young person and want to help kids learn to face their own insecurities and deal with them positively.

The task of establishing belief was not confined to the student population but extended to my administration. My teaching schedule was a combination of choral rehearsal at the middle and high schools, music theory/appreciation class, and one class of instrumental music. A successful and visible choral music program would help insure a full time position. Based on research of more successful programs, we were lacking sufficient training of younger choirs and needed to involve more young men, which is always a challenge because of the changing voice.

Success can be attained when a viable model is followed. There were two keys that launched this program to the next level. First of all, the level and variety of performance had to improve. The level of performance had to become consistent from year to year. Following my first year, our veteran band director and good friend said, "Well, you had a great year. The only problem is, next year they [the public] will expect better". What a challenge: duplicate success. What was it that got us to the level we were? The determination to improve as a musician and conductor was a strong motivation. As does athletics, a music program places a school in front of a community and often becomes a measuring tool for comparison between other school districts. Not only did the public begin evaluating the choir by comparison, but the students began comparing themselves with other school choirs as well. Rising to the challenge of musical excellence in performance served to increase my perseverance.

In order to compete at a new level, the program needed to also increase the number of participants, including male singers. Therefore, I decided to make choir one of the most popular groups at school that students could be involved.

For Reflection...
> *"Any undertaking that will truly make a difference is never a solitary journey."*—Arden Gilmer

Taking Leadership to Heart

Richard Boyatzis at the Weatherhead School of Management at Case Western University in Cleveland, Ohio, has worked with executive development programs for more than thirty years. Through extensive scientific investigation and reflection, he has produced a framework for leadership development. It is based on five discoveries. These are:

76

- The discovery of my ideal self as a leader
- The discovery of my real self as a leader
- The discovery of a plan to develop my leadership
- The discovery of ways to practice good leadership consistently
- The discovery that I need people to help me at every step.

The First Discovery: *My Ideal Self as a Leader* – Who do I want to be? For Christian leaders, this is born out of call, character, and natural competencies. It is in this step that personal vision unfolds. It is a discovery that motivates a person to develop leadership abilities. It is seeing the person you want to be, the person God made you to be. Sometimes this comes through a dream, sometimes through getting in touch with values and commitments that guide your life, through spiritual reflection, through the image of your passion and hope, and through an encounter with the Spirit of God. It is this discovery that will drive you to face and continue in the difficult and often frustrating process of change.

The Second Discovery: *My Real Self as a Leader* – Who am I? What are my strengths and gaps? This is the difficult discovery of looking in the mirror to see who you actually are now – How you act, how others view you, and what comprises your deep beliefs. It often calls for times of personal assessment as well as professional assessment. It involves looking at inner wounds, personal limitations, and the deep beliefs (true or false) that guide your life. This is a soul-searching experience.

The Third Discovery: *A Plan to Develop My Leadership* – How can I build on my strengths while reducing my gaps? It is not enough to simply recognize that "I need to change." People need a plan of action. It is a plan that must be constructed that provides detail guidance on what new things to try each day, building on strengths and moving closer to the ideal. The plan must feel intrinsically satisfying, fitting the learning preferences as well as the realities of life and walk. In essence, this is where a person struggles with the hard task of developing a "personal curriculum" for effective leadership.

The Fourth Discovery: *Ways to Practice Good Leadership Consistently* – Experimenting with and practicing new behaviors, thoughts, and feelings to the point of mastery. It is at this point that developing leaders especially need mentors, professional advisors, spiritual directors, and peer accountability that is thoughtful and encouraging.

The Fifth Discovery: *People to Help Me at Every Step* – Developing supportive and trusting relationships that make change possible. This may occur at any point in the process. It is the discovery that *you need others* to identify your ideal self or find your real self; to discover your strengths and gaps; to help you develop an agenda for your future; and to experiment and practice with timely and helpful feedback, support, and accountability. Leadership development can only occur in the tumult and possibilities of our relationships. Others help developing leaders see things they are missing affirm whatever progress they have made, test their perceptions, and let them know how they are doing. They provide the context for experimentation and practice. Although the model is called a *self-directed learning process,* it actually cannot be done alone. Without others' involvement, lasting change can't occur. And, it is from others that developing leaders receive the recognition for their personal and corporate ministries that they need as they continue to grow and change.

For Reflection...
"Successful leadership doesn't happen in isolation. It is only through the diversity of people bringing together thoughts, ideas, stories of successes and failures, can we grow and develop as leaders."—Vickie Taylor

Learning Exercise #7:
Stories from the Journey

As you read the stories in this chapter, consider two questions:

- What is the passion, what is the plan, and who are the people that help this leader develop?

- How does this person's leadership development express their unique personality and situation?

Story 1:

Story 2:

Story 3:

Story 4:

Story 5:

Story 6:

Learning Exercise #8:
Leadership Development in the Classroom

Divide the class in groups of three or four students. Explain the five discoveries in developing leadership. Assign one of the stories/reflections in this chapter to each group. Ask the groups to read the story.

In group discussion, ask them to fill in what they know about each discovery for the story/reflection they have read. Ask:

- What do you believe is this person's ideal picture of what they want to be as a leader?

- From what you have read and can surmise, what is the real picture of this person's leadership?

- Determine, to the best of your ability, the plan employed by the individual to develop leadership.

- How did they practice the new leadership skills and character qualities they wanted to develop?

- List the supporting relationships that helped this leader develop and grow.

Each story provides more data toward some questions and not others. However, ask each group to "put down something for each of the five discoveries." If there is nothing in the story that is explicit, ask them to make a "smart guess."

As groups report the findings of their discussions, lead the class in exploring the meaning and the means of working through the five discoveries toward leadership development.

Learning Exercise #9:
Leadership Development in Your Organization

To develop leadership in your organization, you can use the information in this chapter for an excellent one - two hour training session.

Begin by explaining the importance of leadership development and the five discoveries that frame a journey toward leadership development.

Then, put your large group into small groups of three or four people. Give each group a set of stories from the chapter. (Choose three stories that best fit your organization.) Ask people to read the stories and underline phrases that they identify with. Have them share these phrases with the group, explaining why they identify with certain phrases. As they listen to each other, there may be additional phrases that they want to include in their own list.

Now, have each person take their list of phrases and categorize them by one of the five discoveries.

- What phrases best fit the "ideal self" discovery?

- What phrases fit the "real self" discovery?

Allow them to share their results with one another. There may be phrases they choose to move from one category to another or a particular phrase that fits in more than one category.

Finally, ask people to look over their list and see what is missing. Let each person develop a personal action plan to work on the one discovery that they believe is most important to them right now.

Leadership Exercise #10:
Leadership Development from a Biblical Base

Explain the five discoveries in leadership development. Choose a biblical character and ask the class what they know about character for each discovery. Do your homework; be ready to lead the discussion.

Then, you can assign a character for a group to investigate. In some cases, the Bible gives enough information to give an extensive commentary on each discovery. Such characters include:

Moses

David

Paul

Other characters will not have as much biblical information but may be just as valuable for exploration. If there is not explicit information on a particular discovery, ask the person to make a "smart guess." In this way, you are helping them reflect on that discovery in the light of their own understanding, a biblical character, and their leadership development.

Learning Exercise #11:
For Personal Leadership Character Development

This exercise will help you develop leadership through the five discoveries. Think through and write out your findings.

• Begin by developing a picture of your ideal self. Ask: What do I really want to be as a leader?
- Deal with what others would like you to be that may not fit your own ideal.
- Search the Scripture for examples of the leadership characteristics that you would like to express.
- How do these character qualities fit with your life mission and goals?
- What are the driving passions and the sense of calling that God has placed on your life?

• What is your real leadership character at this time? This is a tough question to answer. It involves potential, gaps, and strengths.
- It means looking at your potential. You cannot be someone else. You can be the best person that is inside of you.
- It also means looking at your gaps. There are places where you are not what you would like to be someday.
- Finally, it also means taking stock of your strengths. Building on these will give you a greater potential for success.

- **What is your plan for development?** Everybody plans in a little different way.
    - You may be a visionary person who then seizes every opportunity to make things work toward your vision.
    - You may be a strategic person who really likes a clear plan with definite action steps and measurable goals.
    - Or, you may be a free-spirited person who has a set of principles and likes to keep the rest of the future open to opportunity.
    - You need to plan in a way that works for you. But, your plan will be better if you have some goals and actions that you can pursue.

- **Where will you practice your new character qualities?** Leaders tend to perform rather than practice.
    - Find the other areas in your life that are open for you to practice new character qualities.
    - For example, If you want to be more understanding of others, there may be opportunities to get involved in your church, to volunteer at a homeless shelter, or even to become more understanding in your family.
    - Where is a safe place for you to practice better leadership?

- **Who are the people that you need?** Here, you must be specific and clear.
    - Do you need a mentor?
    - Do you need a spiritual director?
    - Do you need a professional advisor?
    - Who are the people that you need, and where will you find them?

Chapter 4
The Leader/Teacher: Inviting Others to Share the Trip

Noel M. Tichy from the University of Michigan in his book, *The*

Leadership Engine: How Winning Companies Build Leaders at Every

Level (New York: HarperBusiness, 1997), defines great leaders as great

teachers. It is not enough to learn to lead; you must teach others to lead.

The "leader/teacher" develops the whole organization by raising the

quantity and quality of leaders in the organization. This pattern is very

similar to that given by the Apostle Paul to the Ephesians when he

described the work of the "pastor/teacher":

> *"...to prepare God's people for works of service, so that*
> *the body of Christ may be built up until we all reach*
> *unity in the faith and in the knowledge of the Son of God*
> *and become mature, attaining to the whole measure of*
> *the fullness of Christ."* (Ephesians 4:12-13)

If I were to paraphrase this passage in terms of modern

leadership theory, it might read: We are to mentor servant-leaders so

that the whole organization may be built up until all reach unity in the vision and values as well as the knowledge that this is a worthwhile enterprise, and people become mature, growing in every dimension of their lives – physically, socially, relationally, intellectually, and spiritually."

To be a leader/teacher, a good mentor, is to guide individuals toward the five discoveries of leadership development:

- Discovering a picture of your ideal self – the kind of leader you want to be.

- Discovering a picture of your real self – the kind of leader you are, which includes limitations, strengths, and shortcomings.

- Discovering a personal plan to bridge the gap between the real and ideal self.

- Discovering ways to practice new leadership character and finding safe places to test, reflect on, and hone leadership character.

- Discovering that you need people to help you at every step of the way.

It is an intellectual exercise to outline the five discoveries. That's the easy part. The challenge for mentoring is motivating individuals to develop leadership character by working through the five discoveries. .

Motivating Leadership Development

Motivation is a result of personal choice. When a person is forced to take "the required class, yields to the demands of a boss, or is pressured by the "expectations of others," there is not enough motivation to sustain new learning. For a person to be motivated to change, the

88

learning has to be tied to deeper passions. It has to be connected to what they care about at the "gut level."

For you to be a leader/teacher, you must also be motivated to teach and mentor others. This does not come naturally for all leaders. To learn and sustain the leadership quality of developing others, it must be rooted in your deepest passion, your most profound concerns.

Developing leadership in others will not work for you if it is "one more thing" that you, as a leader, have to do. Developing others must become one of only two or three goals that receive your focus as a leader. Developing leadership in others must express your passion, or it will simply be a passing phase.

In this chapter, we will look at these concerns: Who is a leader/teacher? What is the relationship between the leader/teacher and a follower? And, how does a leader design a plan for developing others.

For Reflection...
"In leading others you become vulnerable."
—Valerie A. Farmer

Who is a Leader/Teacher?

LeBron Fairbanks, President of Mt. Vernon Nazarene College, and Marc Farmer, Chief Inspector of Judicial Protective Services for the United States Marshals Service, offer two pathways to tap in to your passion for developing others. LeBron Fairbanks gives a biblical framework that reveals his inner vision for developing leadership character in others. Marc Farmer takes a contemporary situation and digs out the principles that hold him steady in the midst of crisis. These principles form the basis for mentoring others.

For Reflection...

"I believe that "integrity" is the one characteristic that allows leaders to flow into the level of service that is necessary to give people the confidence they need to follow their leader."—C. Jay Matthews

"MENTORING LEADERSHIP CHARACTER"
E. LeBron Fairbanks
President, Mt. Vernon Nazarene College

Jesus challenges us in Luke 6:40, "When a student is fully trained he will become like his teacher." (Or his school president, or his seminary professor, or his pastor!) Ministry is always incarnated and enfleshed. Ministry must be lived out!

What is it about ourselves that we want our community—our students and faculty, or our parishioners—to catch from us? We want our people to catch from us a servant spirit, committed to *motivating, equipping* and *enabling others to also serve in Jesus' name.*

What we are confronted with is the need to communicate a lifestyle within the community that is distinctly Christian – and self-giving at the core. But how do you communicate a lifestyle? How do you teach commitments, priorities, values, and spiritual disciplines? How do you teach a lifestyle?

Whatever else it means, it demands taking seriously the principle of imitation. Herbert Mayer, in his book, *Pastoral Care, Its Roots and Renewal*, reminds us that this principle was a key in Christian leadership for eighteen centuries. We must recapture this principle if we take

90

seriously the biblical mandate to be mentors and examples to believers. Recall the words of the Apostle Paul:

- Follow me as I follow Christ.
- You ought to follow my example.
- Put into practice what you have learned, received or heard from me or seen in me.
- We did this in order to make ourselves a model for you to follow.

Paul gave these instructions with humility to the Christians under his care. We must do the same for those for whom we are responsible.

The broad principle of imitation must <u>possess</u> us if we are to effectively <u>transfer</u> our vision, passion, and obsession within the Christian fellowship. This principle is developed and made specific in Ephesians 4:25-32. The passage outlines a mentoring leadership lifestyle within the Christian community.

Ephesians, Chapter four begins with the challenge to walk worthy of our calling as Christians. The characteristics of the person "walking worthy" follow the challenge. We are instructed to be gentle, humble, patient, and supportive of each other. In so living, we will "maintain the unity of the spirit in the bond of peace" (v.3).

But, as Christian leaders, how do we express <u>gentleness</u>, <u>humbleness</u>, <u>patience</u>, and <u>supportiveness</u>? The key leadership principle <u>captivating</u> the leader in community is found in Ephesians 4:15 – "speak the truth in love," and this critical concept is fleshed out in verses 25-32.

Paul, in these verses, is not so much talking about administrative techniques, but Christian attitudes underlying our actions and activities within the community. We are co-laborers together in the body of Christ (v. 25). We relate with others in the fellowship out of an "I-Thou" frame of reference. The people with whom we work are God's own creation.

Because of this fundamental Christian conviction, we can *be honest*…with the believers; *immediate*…in dealing with conflict among us; *upbuilding*…with our words; and *forgiving*, even when others do not forgive us.

91

We express, therefore, gentleness, humbleness, patience, and supportiveness through words and deeds that consistently communicate these leadership character imperatives:

I love you, I accept you, I respect you, I need you, I trust you, I serve you, I forgive you, and I accept your forgiveness.

Words and deeds done by others to us must never be permitted to create bitterness and resentment within us.

An obsession for community is not an option for the mentoring leader. It is an imperative, even in conflictual situations. Because relationships are so important to us, we "care enough to confront" our brother or sister in Christ. We are too much about the relationship to ignore destructive behavior. We speak the truth in love, and we care enough to allow our brother or sister in Christ to speak truthfully to us.

Paul's instructions are not psychological in nature; they are deeply theological. The Spirit of God is deeply concerned with the speech of His people (Eph. 4:30a).

These instructions may not be found in the latest secular textbook on leadership. They are foundational for servant leaders who take seriously the principle of imitation, and who want their faith community to catch from them a servant spirit.

STRENGTHS AND CRISIS OF LEADERSHIP CHARACTER
Marc Farmer
Chief Inspector, Judicial Protective Services
United States Marshals Service

It's 9:00 a.m., Monday morning. Your mind is sharp and crisp and ready to conquer the world. Your recent promotion has boosted your self-confidence. Oh, and the congratulations you received from co-workers, the vote of confidence, "Hand in there; Don't let us down; You deserve to be on the top!" It's now 10:45 a.m. and you are summoned to "Mahogany Row." Your promotion has now landed you where you always wanted to be, face-to-face with the CEO. What an opportunity to launch your great ideas.

92

The CEO begins the meeting patting you on the back, while breaking the news to you. The Board of Directors has decided to downsize because of the economy, talk of a recession. Your job is to lay off some workers in your division of which you were promoted to lead. The CEO says to you, I know you will not have a problem making the hard decisions, we only want the top-producers. Reduce your division by 25 percent. He places a list of employees before you, and says, "I want them gone. I want people who know how to make a sales quota, especially when the chips are down". Reviewing the list, you see the names of some of your top workers, the persons who put in an honest day's work. It does not seem fair. The ethical and moral are among the first to be laid-off. Others who have been warned over the years about unethical sales practices get to stay. What should you do? Besides you just got promoted, bought a new car, put your old house on the market.

While listening to the CEO tell you, you are a great team player. There's a lot at stake to include personal risk. Is it a matter of principle or your pocket or purse? Every leader will be faced with a leadership challenge—a crisis. Being a leader is never an isolated subject. It always involves a series of decisions impacting others and yourself. Listed are some things a leader must consider:

1) Use of time in making a leadership decision—too often leaders think they have to make snap decisions. The quicker, the better the leader you are. This is not true. There are a lost of leadership decisions which are important. Few are urgent! If time is used properly in making a leadership decision, it's a strength not a weakness.

2) Properly understanding the scope of the problem—failing to understand the dimension of a problem and the context in which it must be solved can become a crisis, which can lead to decision paralysis.

3) Knowing when to release or hold on to an issue, idea or project for the greater good of all—learning this is a strength, failing to learn it is a weakness.

4) Avoiding the leadership trap—no leader is perfect, flawless— There is no such thing as absolute leadership perfection. Striving for leadership perfection is a process of growth, not an event. Leaders learn to accept setbacks and build upon successes and failures. Failing as a leader does not mean 'you' the person

has failed—try a new approach—failures are often some stepping stones, a process in finding the right way to success.

5) Avoid fatal optimism—learn to convey optimistic realism—forget about the "rose-colored glasses" of optimism. Don't ignore the reality of any situation. With every crisis there comes opportunity.

6) Avoid Compartmentalizing your life beliefs—too often leaders attempt to divide up their world into a false dichotomy between the spiritual and the secular—this is impossible and dangerous, and ultimately leads to character erosion and fatal compromise. Character is an imprint upon the heart putting into motion operating convictions, which dictate behavior and thought.

7) Leaders must understand and rely on the sufficiency of God's grace as the source of their strength, a very present help in the time of trouble.

Lastly, all leaders are mentors whether they are cognizant of it or not. Mentoring is the process of carrying the lighted torch and passing it to another while the flame is still lit.

For Reflection...
"Integrity can only develop in a setting where a leader is willing to relinquish his/her freedom."
—Bill Perkins

The Relationship of the Leader/Teacher and Follower

Larita Hand, executive director of Mercy Ministries, and Mary

Kaufmann, Director of Sales Development for the Longaberger Basket

Company, give two views of the relationship between the mentor and the

mentoree or the leader/teacher and the developing leader. These articles

describe a unique relational quality and the significance of spirituality in the process. Also, note that both writers are focused on the process rather than the outcome.

Guiding a person's leadership development means helping them make discoveries. They discover a vision for themselves. They discover where they are currently and what it would take to make a change. They discover how they can learn these new patterns of thinking and relating. And, they discover people they need to help them. Each discovery is like a new treasure.

The task driven leader is more focused on outcome than process, on results rather than relationships. The task driven leader is tempted to give the colleague the discovery they need—to tell their colleague what their vision and plan should be.

You cannot discover something for someone else. You can only open a process in which they have the possibility of making the discovery.

For Reflection...
> *"As leaders we can become competent in skills and knowledge, and while this is an important aspect of leadership, it will not pass the test of time."*
> —Mike Little

"MENTORING LEADERSHIP CHARACTER IN OTHERS"
Larita Hand
Executive Director, Mercy Ministries

Mercy Missions Inc. is an interfaith ministry to the brokenhearted and missions to those that are hungry desolate in their environment, minds and spirit. In my field we train and equip leaders in leadership character development to enable them to minister to health and healing to those who desire to be made whole through the Word of God.

We mentor our leaders within the organization. We attempt to fulfill these areas in the mentoring process to assist them in Leadership Character; core values, establishment and fulfillment of ministry goals, formation of spirituality in their lives, conflict resolution, self-evaluation inventory and building trust with their teammates.

The crisis in the field is the inability of the mentor to maintain a relationship that is free from competition with the mentee. The mentor can become absorbed with the needs of the mentee that the mentor lacks discretion when to release the mentee to grow.
I have mentored people that desire to become copycats of my personality to avoid facing their own personal challenges in Leadership Character development. When this behavior is displayed by the mentee I often suggest to them to find another mentor different from my personality type to help the mentee to face their own challenges.

In my field of ministry I provide Pastoral Counseling through Mercy Missions Inc. for those who desire the service. In the case of a particular crisis with a leader, I provide the same service to them to help them identify their inability to wrestle with the process of development of Leadership Character. Leaders have difficulty admitting to their character flaws. It is important to them that when they divulge their issues with me that they know that I have taken a vow of confidentiality and my position in those times is to assist them with the struggle in moral, ethical and spiritual issues in Leadership.

My approach to mentoring is to build an honest and trusty relationship with the mentee. I share with the mentee my life experiences and the challenges. In addition I attempt to spend quality time with the mentee in a familiar environment, such as their home, or sharing a meal in my home and encouraging them by attending some event in their life that is important to them.

The ministry provides travel opportunities to local missions as well as international missions. I usually share a room with a woman mentee on mission assignment to learn how they function in personal space. The mentee and I usually develop a bond of trust and confidence in each other through sharing personal space together. I encourage the mentee to become a mentor to someone new in ministry to keep the process of development of Leadership Character as a life goal.

For Reflection...
> *"Leadership isn't selling ideas, it's developing others."*—Donnette Smith

"MENTORING LEADERSHIP CHARACTER IN OTHERS"
Mary Kaufmann
Director, Sales Development
Longaberger Company

All around me, people are going through great change, ranging from dealing with global issues, to increased demands at work and in their family lives. The visible strength is the great effort being put forth to adapt their lives to gain some sense of order. People are seeking to improve their circumstances and ultimately their quality of life.

The crisis in this effort is the lack of knowledge, ability and experience or how to manage these changes. The values that were known to be a true part of their world and therefore part of their "worth" are disappearing. People need to see progress while they attempt to navigate through this time of change. In an age when technology is changing at an exponential rate, people need to feel as though their efforts are valued and that their contributions have substance; they are seeking to be a part of something meaningful and worthwhile.

People need a solid rock from which to position the fulcrum to balance these great changes. Understanding the root of the problem is the place to start in addressing the crisis. People need a clear mission of where they are going in life and how to get there. The great philosopher, Augustine reminds us, "There is a God shaped vacuum inside the heart of every man that cannot be filled by any created thing but only by God the father made known through Jesus Christ." When people are separated from God, they are naturally unable to feel complete. My mission, therefore, is to introduce each searching soul to the only One who can make them complete…Jesus Christ.

I have become comfortable telling the good news of Jesus with everyone and anyone with whom I come into contact. My faith, and how it has changed my life, has become a natural part of my conversation and my way of life.

My faith has given me the gift of peace at the very core of my being. During times of great stress, I can calmly address and resolve issues because I am not working alone, but with God. I have had people ask me how I remain calm and this question brings an opportunity to share my faith. People are drawn to calm and confident behavior. They want to learn how to acquire this skill.

When people come to me for advice, I usually ask them if they have prayed and asked for guidance. If they have not yet prayed, I offer to pray with them right there on the spot, rather than offering a glib, "I'll be praying for you." I seek an answer in prayer first, then provide guidance. I almost always grab my Bible and read Scripture that seems relevant to their need. I can't count the number of times I suggest they read a passage or book in the Bible and they come back to talk to me about the application of that particular passage of Scripture in their life.

When I read a good book about faith and it's transforming power, I buy many copies and give them to specific people in need. People will rarely buy a recommended book, but when they receive it as a gift they seem much more likely to read it!

I have made a habit of praying for my 'enemies' and leading others to do the same. I pray in all things for God's will to be done and I suggest others do the same.

I have reached out to every Christian I know in the workplace and we meet regularly to pray for our company, the leadership, all employees and our customers. We pray for many things including direction and discernment especially in the midst of turbulent times.

> *"Being a leader means being "out there"—*
> *taking risks by modeling integrity, being put to the test*
> *yourself, and living with the consequences (with the*
> *grace of God)."*—Lisa Berlinger

The challenge for the leader/teacher is moving his or her focus from achieving results to a more uncommon focus of empowering others. In doing this a leader is moving from task to people orientation, from solving problems in the organization to helping others solve their own problems, from determining goals to helping others discover their own goals, from commanding to inspiring. The leader moves his or her eye from short-term returns to long-term growth. And becomes a masterful leader/teacher.

How to Design a System for Developing Others?

Charles Lake, pastor of Greenwood Community Church, and Rod Bushey, high school choral director, offer two ways for designing systems and structures that will develop leaders. Charles Lake takes the programmatic approach, seeking to mentor one-on-one, offering classes for leadership development, and facilitating small mentoring groups. Rod Bushey, on the other hand, describes how mentoring is built into the structure of his organization. In fact, he views the purpose of his organization as developing leadership character in high school students.

These approaches are complementary. There can be specific programs designed to enrich leadership development. And, the system and structure of the organization can be designed so that mentoring one another becomes natural, expected, and part of the organizational culture.

As you read these articles, ask yourself these questions: What programs do we have in place for developing leadership character; what programs do we need in order to develop leadership character in others? How does our system encourage people to mentor one another; how does our system discourage people from mentoring one another?

For Reflection...

> *"It's OK. It's OK to be me. It's OK to trust that God can take me, just as I am, just where I am, and use me to do this work."*—Jay Brooks

MENTORING DEVLOPES LEADERS
Charles Lake
Founding Pastor, Greenwood Community Church

While sad but true "mentoring" is a relatively new concept within the church. Most writings on the topic date back to the early 1990's. Only in recent years have colleges, universities and seminaries devoted resources to develop schools of leadership development and has the topic become a part of the seminary curriculum.

Growing churches have also necessitated the need for leadership development. Pastors have come to realize they can't do the task alone and for years they have overlooked the untapped resources of trainable laity who are ready to be challenged with ministry. More and more larger churches are spending time and resources on the assimilation of members not only into the membership but also the ministry of the church.

Over the past few years I have addressed the issue in our local congregation in several ways. First, by a commitment to mentor existing staff in hope of supplicating in them the mentoring vision. Adopting the promise that we will not ask anyone in our organization to undertake any task we are not ready to train them to do has produced some significant challenges. More and more, I am surrounding myself with staff who are not only committed but who are competent to mentor others.

An annual leadership training class is a given. Potential leaders are personally invited to attend while the class is open to any who desire to be included. Eighteen weeks of material is disseminated and the progress of each participant is monitored. A system of trying new leaders in lesser roles in order to evaluate their potential for greater responsibility is also being implemented.

On a weekly basis I meet with eight men who have stated their desire to some day be in the professional ministry. Sharing personal experiences, doing case studies, sharing resources for their consumption, providing some on-the-job training opportunities are a few of the tools used to mentor them. Already sever have taken on greater roles of responsibility within the church.

Mentoring is becoming increasingly a way of life. I find myself more selective in whom I make the greater commitment of my time. I try, as much as possible, not to do any ministry assignment of my own without taking someone along with me to learn by observation and instruction. I presently have two interns on my staff whom I am trying to equip to plant new churches.

Challenging mentorees to read biographies and success stories of other well-known leaders has also enriched their understanding of leadership character. By far the most specific tool in mentoring has been that of accountability. Helping those being mentored to identify their character deficiencies, develop a game plan to address those deficiencies, and hold them accountable to the game plan has been most rewarding. One-on-one or in small groups men and women meet weekly to lovingly confront one another. Accountability is viewed as an essential in the process of building strong leaders.

Any leader may have no greater opportunity than to reproduce himself in the life of someone younger and less experienced. Passing on an honorable legacy of leadership character is a remarkable accomplishment that should challenge any leader.

"...POINT 'EM IN THE RIGHT DIRECTION"
Rod Bushey
High School Choral Director
Howell, Michigan

A motorist drove onto the wrong ramp and entered a busy divided highway going the wrong way. Someone saw him and immediately broadcast a warning on a CB radio: "There's a car going the wrong way on the highway." The mistaken motorist heard the message and quickly replied, "One car going the wrong way! There are hundreds!" "Point 'em in the right direction" was a statement that struck fear in me initially when heard and later served as a welcome challenge. In many ways, I have been in the pointing business for a number of years. My superintendent likes to refer to our choir program as the "pied piper" syndrome. This August began my thirtieth year of teaching and I can certainly say it has been quite a ride. There are many professions out there that bring in more income than education. However, there are few that offer the degree of personal satisfaction found in teaching.

Ownership

Ownership is a concept that has brought energy, pride, and integrity to the choir program. Part of the "pointing" process begins with structuring a leadership scheme within each choir. When the students are involved in the decision process, the recruiting of singers, and the planning of activities and programs, they become enthusiastically involved. Here are some of the positions that encourage ownership of the program. Each area of responsibility has specific tasks to accomplish. Some tasks are ongoing, some are given as the need arises.

President

Each class elects a president who is their leader for the year. They are directed to nominate those who would be a model student both in and away from the classroom. That person should be someone who would represent the choir in the general school climate as an exemplary citizen and be an individual the students respect.

Vice-President

This office not only operates in the absence of the president but is in charge of most social activities of the choir. The V.P. from the oldest choir holds a committee meeting to plan and organize parties, picnics, and hosting choirs and guests from other schools. The group of Vice-Presidents delegate to each choir what they are to bring to the activity and organize set-up, decorating, and clean-up groups.

Secretary

Each class has record keeping and daily attendance taking. The primary job of this person is to make certain attendance is taken. In their absence, one of the other officers will make sure the assignment is completed. The secretary will assist officers with other jobs that need assistance.

Treasurer

One of the most demanding offices is that of treasurer. Each student has an account and when we have a fund raising project, a percentage of everything that students sells goes in an "account" to be used for purchasing concert tapes, tux shirts, tour fees, choir shirts, etc. This needs to be kept up to date after each fundraiser and each time a purchase is made, the treasurer records the deposits and deductions to and from each student's account. Also, at the beginning of each year, the treasurer with the most seniority holds a workshop one day after school and explains the procedure to the new treasurers.

Program and Publicity

These positions are among the most visible areas that come in contact with the public. The program position is assigned and not elected. This appointed office is a junior or senior along with an apprentice to learn how the concert programs are produced. They are responsible to spell names correctly, proof the final copies, and get the master copy to the print shop.

At the end of the year, we produce a 30-40 page booklet titled the "A cappella Annual" that consists of mock elections, senior wills, and...in twenty years section. The annual was initiated and produced by the students. Please understand that I become the editor of each program and censor of the annual to protect the integrity of the project.

Because of the number of students in the program, it has become less important that we advertise the concerts. We seat around 1,050 in the auditorium and aggressively advertise only two concerts each year because we cannot seat everyone comfortably. The publicity chairpersons operate out of a committee and are in charge of bulletin boards and showcases that promote the pride and accomplishments of the choir. It becomes important that we keep the community and school aware of the choir's success. Keeping the choir visible promotes a positive atmosphere among the membership.

Robarians

Although my computer does not recognize the word "robarian", the need to inventory the robes that uniform two of the choirs is the responsibility of these officers. They make sure everyone is assigned a robe, the length is correct, and the stoles are in good shape. If they need dry cleaning or pressing, they arrange for those needs. This job is not elected by assigned by director's approval.

Librarians

With the amount of music issued prior to the four major concerts, tours, solo and ensemble and choral festivals, this position is overwhelming and the responsibility of more than one person. This job is also assigned along with an apprentice. The library is catalogued on computer and all the music boxed and filed.

When asked why I do not have a "Parent's Booster" group, I find it more beneficial to keep the students involved in the operation of the total program. Parents have been most helpful and supportive across the years. It has been evident that when their children are pleased and involved with the activity at school, more calls to compliment are received in my office as opposed to complaints.

Parental involvement is best as chaperones on tour, festivals, or for parties. They enjoy watching their kids perform and sharing the pride of the program. While on tour, I have a meeting with the chaperones and explain where I need their help. We experience a great feeling of cooperation on tours and at festivals.

"...Get Out of the Way"

When students come in the choir room before or after school, who are "non-members" the standing joke is: "If Mr. Bushey has not asked you why you aren't in choir yet, he will". Recruiting into the program has been done on regular basis, especially regarding young men. Last year, I asked my Men's Choir students to speak to the entire eighth grade and encourage guys to be part of the choir. They auditioned their speeches and six young men were very convincing as they expressed a genuine pride in the program. We recruited about 40 new male voices.

The choir students express a loyalty and pride that has become a part of the conversation. A few weeks ago, the officers asked if they could order sweatshirts with "HHS Choirs" on the front and their name and choirs names on the back. This is not a required purchase, yet most everyone in the choirs has ordered one. They designed an order form, collected and deposited the money, and ordered the shirts. I just got out of the way and let them run with the idea.

We began a few years ago with four choirs and about one hundred singers. Today, we have nine choirs and four hundred forty singers. Two ensembles rehearse one afternoon each week with students running the rehearsals. They are responsible for selecting music, writing it in some cases, choreographing the appropriate selections, and booking performances throughout the community.

Connecting with the students is the greatest satisfaction I have experienced. A program of this size is still made up of individuals. We became successful one at a time. Encouraging students to improve their own musicality became a major factor that improved the ensembles in which they sang. They improved their music reading as ensemble members and studied voice to expand their vocal ability. When they became successful in solo performance, we gained strength and quality in the larger choirs.

They have become a group of students leading students. Our slogan is hoisted high above the students and reads: "In Pursuit of Excellence". We promote excellence in performance, rehearsal, discipline, responsibility, attitude, relationships, and oh yes, leadership. I am much richer today because of my involvement with the students at Howell High School. Someday I plan on retiring from my current responsibility, but until that happens, we will continue to pursue excellence in choral music while "pointing and then getting out of the way".

For Reflection...

> *"The most important lesson I take home from today is confirmation of the importance of passion, vision, integrity, and competence to leadership character. And, the reminder that accountability structures, disciplines, and perseverance are crucial to maintaining leadership character."*—Lovett H. Weems, Jr.

In any program you design, you have to find a way to help people make that first discovery – the ideal self. You must help people dig through all the layers of expectations and find again that inner vision for what they believe they can be. You have got to go to the heart of leadership for that person. In the next chapter, you will see a process for helping people discover a personal vision for leadership.

Learning Exercise #12:
A Vision for a Leader/Teacher

In order to develop leaders in your organization, you will need to tap into your own passion for developing leaders. To do that:

- Write out your vision and your principles for developing leadership character in others.

- Share your vision and principles with at least three trusted friends who can help you reflect on and refine them.

- Determine what leadership character you need to fulfill your vision and principle statements.

- Develop a clear and actionable plan for becoming a leader/teacher.

- List the support of good people who can encourage, assess, and guide you.

Clarity in your passion for developing others is essential. As other people experience your passion to see them grow and develop, it will help them hook into their deep concerns and motivating passions of their life. This is a great source of growth.

Learning Exercise #13:
Relationships with a Leader/Teacher

To develop the mindset and relational paradigm needed to develop leadership character in others, ask yourself the following questions:

- To what degree can you trust the process; to what degree do you need to control the outcome?

- To what degree can you accept the person(s) unconditionally; to what degree do you find yourself evaluating or judging them?

- To what degree can you help people make valuable discoveries for their own growth; to what degree do you need the discoveries to have a "payoff" for your own agenda?

- To what degree can you release the person(s) as they grow and develop; to what degree do you need to own the person as they grow and develop?

After you have done your best to answer these questions for yourself, arrange for three or four conversations with people you trust; people who know you and are willing to tell you the truth. Take them through the same series of questions and ask them to be open and honest with you. Also, ask them for two or three things you could start doing now that would help you become a better leader/teacher.

Learning Exercise #14:
A Support Structure for Developing Leaders

You will want to consider both of these approaches to increasing leadership development in your organization.

Adjust the System.

Talk to people in your organization and ask them this question, "Who in this organization was the greatest help to you in developing as a leader?" When you gather a group of names, call them together and talk about how the way organization works either enhances or discourages mentoring one another. Out of the discussion, determine two or three action steps you can take to make your organization more "mentor friendly."

Design a Program.

Go back to your vision and principles. If you were to design a program to teach this vision and these principles, how would you do it? Are you better at one-on-one conversations? Do you like to facilitate a small group? Do you like to teach in a class setting? As you are designing your program, keep in mind the five discoveries that people must make if they're going to develop leadership character: My ideal self, my real self, my plan to change, my place to practice, and the people that will support me.

Chapter 5
My Destination: The Leader I Want To Be

When a person connects with their dream, it releases energy, excitement, and passion about life. The key to discovering your ideal self, the leader you would like to be, is reaching down to the gut level.

In this chapter, nine leaders from different walks of life share their personal "gut level" search for the heart of leadership. Khushwant Pittenger, Chair of the Undergraduate Business Program and Professor of Business Administration of Ashland University, describes the experience of self-discovery that took place at the Roundtable in October 2001:

> *A leader's character is the heart of leadership. But,*
> *what is character? Character is who you are, not what*
> *others think you are or what you want others to think*
> *you are or what you are in public or in private but who*
> *you are in your entirety. How many of us, when we are*
> *being brutally truthful, know who we are? Or, are we*
> *truly who we think we are? At this convocation, I was*
> *fortunate enough to share the Roundtable with*
> *participants who were courageous enough to share their*
> *struggle with their own personal "self-discovery."*
> *Getting to know one's true self is a noble goal, but it is a*
> *hard journey. I am heartened to know that I am not*
> *alone in this struggle.*

Taking time to consider who you are and who you can become can be a source of hope and worry. The worry settles over the obstacles on the pathway. There is an initial feeling of excitement about an ideal future. However, enthusiasm often fades. People become frustrated with the fact that they are not already living the dream.

Hope makes the difference. You have to consistently and vividly imagine how great it will be on the day you reach the goal. You must fixate on that hope:

> *Keep your eyes on Jesus, who both began and finished this race we're in. Study how he did it. Because he never lost sight of where he was headed—that exhilarating finish in and with God—he could put up with anything along the way: cross, shame, whatever. And now he's there, in the place of honor, right alongside God. When you find yourselves flagging in you faith, go over that story again, item by item, that long litany of hostility he plowed through. That will shoot adrenaline into your souls!*—Hebrews 12:2-3 from the message.

If you fasten your attention to the obstacles in your way, you will plunge yourself into a pessimistic view that will steal your motivation to grow and change. The first mental habit you need on the path of character development is hope that overcomes pessimism.

Daniel Goleman, Richard Boyatzis, and Annie McKee, in their book Primal Leadership (Harvard Business School Press, 2001), reflect on the obstacles to growth. They begin with the "ought" self. This "ought" self" is the person you think you should become. Max Weber, the sociologist, calls it the "iron cage." You find yourself trapped when you see your ideal self slipping from view. Your vision becomes fuzzy, and your dream evaporates like morning fog. Pressure from life's responsibilities can make you numb to your passion.

Another obstacle to overcome is the fact that dreams and aspirations change as life unfolds. You may find yourself straying from your calling just because you keep on doing the same thing, ignoring the changes in your core values. From all outward appearance, it seems that you are a leader of character, but there is a level of inauthenticity slipping into the foundation of your soul. It is a first step toward compromising character.

The way to overcome obstacles is to keep the ideal image in view – See the leader you want to be. This is how you engage your passion, emotion, and motivation. Your personal vision is the deepest expression of what you want in life. That image becomes a guide for your decisions and a barometer for your sense of satisfaction.

When you get hold of that vision, it will bring you courage and commitment. You will have the courage to stand up for what you are, what you are becoming, and what you know is the right thing. It will give you commitment to stay with it through the hard decisions, the challenges of compromise, and the tough times.

For Reflection...
>   *The most important lesson I take home from today is the conviction that heart is the source of a leader's character."*—Rick Ryding

THE HEART OF LEADERSHIP CHARACTER
Jayne L. Cooper
President of the Ashland Area Chamber of Commerce

I now begin my fifth pass at this essay. And that is somewhat uncommon as I can usually "flow" when I sit at a keyboard and focus. I can only hope this is the magical time, the last, the most focused, most "this is what I really mean to say" time.

I have been surprised at all the mental paper-crumbling that I have done. First, I tried the definition approach. Define heart, character, leadership. By the end of several pages, I was sure I had not even skimmed the surface of the heart of character leadership. The essay was almost abstract, and clearly, this topic cannot be mined from the outside.

Somewhere in the drafts, I cited character leadership examples: experiences of my own leadership (good and not-even-close), examples from leaders I have observed and those reported of leaders. These chronicles skirted the topic at best, for even in my own citations, they were almost third person. Again, external in nature.

I keep wanting to go deeper, for as we have all discovered somewhere when thinking about character leadership, we settle on the reality that this is a topic that demands reaching deep inside our own heart. Leadership comes in many forms, but the exercise of defining the heart of character leadership becomes a personal character study.

If you serve as a leader, how you view the crux of the question is how you see yourself as a leader of character. For me, I consider it a continual journey to become the best leader of character that I can be, but again, back to the question, what is at the heart?

Now, in this draft I have finally settled on quotes as a guide to my analysis. I am always moved by the insights of others, those who have learned and will share with the rest of us, their wisdom. I'm excited when someone's understanding makes me pause and think, or centers within me a realism that has been just beyond my grasp.

The Harold W. McGraw, Jr., Prize in Education begins its application with this: "When our children reach for the stars, whose shoulders will they stand on?" Doesn't that say, in so many words, that only leaders of character need apply?

> *"Keep thoughts positive – your thoughts become words,keep words positive – your words become behavior, keep behavior positive – your behavior becomes habit, keep habits positive – your habits become values, keep values positive – your values become destiny."*--Gandhi

Or simply, *"I regret often that I have spoken, never that I have been silent."* Cyrus

Aren't these behaviors for leaders of character to model? The list of quotes that circle around the heart of character leadership are, to me, very similar in nature.

But as I focused more and more, I kept coming back to what the Lord has said about how we treat others, how we serve others, how we look to him as our model, how our character is to be God-centered.

Leadership character, as defined by Dr. Richard Parrott in the preamble of a recent workshop on this subject, is that habit or pattern of behavior that distinguishes one leader from another. Key words are habit and pattern. As they relate to the character of a leader, most would agree that these patterns and habits must be grounded in what is good and right, deep within a leader.

As a Christian, I know that I know that I know, only God can mold character. Only God can set us on, and keep us on, the path that ends with a leader of strong character. Only God can make us a true servant to those who would follow us. When we demonstrate an authentic and genuine desire to help others succeed, then we are exhibiting the heart of character leadership or servanthood.

If the passion of our leadership grows out of God's purpose in that calling, then our motivation will be good and honorable. And if we allow the Lord to shape us, we will be worthy of trust. A quote from Dr. Parrott that stuck with me went something like this. "Leaders that inspire a low level of trust add a tax to everything. Leaders inspiring a high level of trust is like adding a wind at your back." Staying close to God is at the heart of character leadership.

Looking at character leadership another way, I considered this riddle. If you assume someone is a good leader, and you assume then that the leader is also a good person, can you further assume they are a leader of good character? If Jesus is the Lord of the leader, and if the leader allows the Holy Spirit to work within them, I say the answer is yes. Absent these, the answer is not certain.

Let me return to quotes.

David tells us that God himself is character. "He whose walk is blameless and who does what is righteous, who speaks the truth from his heart and has no slander on his tongue, who does his neighbor no wrong and casts no slur on his fellowman, who despises a vile man but honors those who fear the Lord, who keeps his oath even when it hurts, who lends his money without usury and does not accept a bribe against the innocent. He who does these things will never be shaken." Psalm 15:2-5.

Paul told the Philippians that "whatever is true, whatever is noble, whatever is right, whatever is pure, whatever is lovely, whatever is admirable - if anything is excellent or praiseworthy – think about such things. Whatever you have learned or received or heard from me, or seen in me – put it into practice." Philippians 4: 8-9a.

At the heart of character leadership then is patterned behavior that signals in ways big and small, perhaps in ways both inherent as well as intentional, that a leader is a person of integrity that can be trusted. These traits cannot be imposed from the outside, but must be shaped in our very souls. They truly come from the heart, for at the root of character leadership is love, pure and simple. Love of God and love for people.

What is the heart of character leadership? It is not what, I conclude, but who.

For Reflection...
> *"Over these last couple of days, I have been reminded, I am a leader. I am in the position of influencing people. And, this is an overwhelming realization; anxiety producing when I consider what leadership character is all about."*—Bob Rosa

"THE HEART OF LEADERSHIP CHARACTER"
Arden E. Gilmore
Senior Pastor, Park Street Brethren Church

As I reflect on the heart of leadership character based on the input from the Leadership Round Table and observations from my own experience, I've focused on integrity, trustworthiness and the response to these – namely, trust.

"People don't do what you expect; they do what you inspect." When I heard a management expert say these words several years ago, I thought, "That's a very cynical view of human beings." Unfortunately,

116

my experience has verified that this is, indeed, true of many people. However, and gladly so, my experience has also verified that this statement may be true of many people, but certainly not of all.

People without an internal integrity compass may measure up only if there's an external stimulus – someone standing over them, watching their every move, holding them accountable all the time. However, people of integrity have character and an inner motivation that will act according to that character regardless of the existence of or the nature of external stimulation. This character is an 'inside-out' phenomenon succinctly described by the Apostle Peter, "As we know Jesus better, his divine power gives us everything we need for living a godly life. He has called us to receive his own glory and goodness! And by that same mighty power, he has given us all of his rich and wonderful promises. He has promised that you will escape the decadence all around you caused by evil desires and that you will share in his divine nature.

So make every effort to apply the benefits of these promises to your life. Then your faith will produce a life of moral excellence. A life of moral excellence leads to knowing God better. Knowing God leads to self-control. Self-control leads to patient endurance, and patient endurance leads to godliness. Godliness leads to love for other Christians, and finally you will grow to have genuine love for everyone. The more you grow like this, the more you will become productive and useful in your knowledge of our Lord Jesus Christ. But those who fail to develop these virtues are blind or, at least, very shortsighted. They have already forgotten that God has cleansed them from their old life of sin.

So, dear brothers and sisters, work hard to prove that you really are among those God has called and chosen. Doing this, you will never stumble or fall away. And God will open wide the gates of heaven for you to enter into the eternal Kingdom of our Lord and Savior Jesus Christ" (2 Peter 1:3-11NLT).

Someone has said, "Character is what we are in the dark" i.e., when no one is observing us. Integrity is the heart of leadership character. People of character are integrated. A process of growing toward wholeness is happening within them. People of character are authentic and will act on the basis of their character. Their behavior is not based on the nature of the external. They operate based on an 'inner light' even in the dark. There is minimal disconnect or inconsistency between their character and their actions. Because their character is exemplary, people around them trust and respect them. The amount of credibility a leader has is based on the degree to which the followers trust him/her.

I think that, even more than love, trust is the oil that reduces the friction in leader/follower relationships. Paranoia develops in people who are in relationships with people who are not trustworthy. Trustworthiness is an issue of integrity. Trust is the learned response of a person to one whom they know from personal experience to be trustworthy. Leaders of character do not need to demand that they have authority. They know they will, over time, earn the respect of their followers. When that happens, authority has been earned, not demanded. When leaders demand authority, followers often respond with resentment not respect. When leaders earn authority based on their character, followers respond with trust. If the leader is not trustworthy, distrust, skepticism and cynicism will penetrate the relationships of the followers with the leader and even poison the relationships among the followers. This has a negative impact on performance because the people in the organization spend an inordinate amount of energy and time protecting themselves from each other. Distrust produces disharmony. Disharmony destroys teamwork. A lack of teamwork results in lower performance for the entire organization.

However, some people may distrust even the most trust-worthy leader. People raised as children in a dysfunctional atmosphere have imbedded in them the 'rules of dysfunction.' One of these rules is "Don't trust!" Therefore, they engage everyone in their life from the perspective of distrust. They may view with distrust even trustworthy leaders. This can poison all the relationships in which this person is involved. They are always on the defensive, living with their guard up, believing that others are out to get them. They have an uncanny ability to attach all kinds of distrust and suspicion to even the simplest of statements. Thus the distrust felt by some followers may grow more from the woundedness of their own hearts than from the leader's lack of character. For example, Jesus' character is 100 percent pure, and still many of those who follow him, and all of those who do not follow him, distrust him. Why? Their distrust is rooted in their wounded hearts. Couple this with the fact that, because of his/her own woundedness and humanness, no leader's character is 100 percent pure, distrust can, indeed, be a powerful, though negative and unhealthy force.

This presents an obvious and powerful dilemma and raises the question, "Is trust possible?" The answer is a conditional "Yes." The condition? Trust can be, will be, a reality given a transformation of the hearts of both the leaders and the followers through an experience of the healing of their heart wounds through the transforming love, grace, mercy, and power that comes through trust in Jesus. This transformation often begins with an initial transforming event (i.e, new birth), but must also be an ongoing process in which both leaders and followers join hearts and minds as fellow travelers in this process of following Christ together, growing in Him toward wholeness.

For Reflection...
> *"God needs leaders to once again embrace the call of God, rediscovering the courage that comes from the throne of God and never letting go of God's hand."*
> —Marc A. Farmer

THE HEART OF LEADERSHIP CHARACTER
Bill Harris
Senator, 19th Ohio Senate District

The Round Table Convocation, focusing on Leadership Character, October 25-27, 2001 in the Sandberg Leadership Center, Ashland Theological Seminary in Ashland, Ohio was a well structured and designed presentation, study, evaluation, testing and discussion of Leadership Character and the relationship of the Leader's faith in God.

Throughout our small group discussions and structured presentations it was obvious that practically all attendees, if not all, based on their experiences, agreed that God was the source of the leaders ability to successful influence other to follow him/her in accomplishing a mission or objective. Specifically, the leader's **PERSONAL VISION** for his/her life accepts that God is in control and their faith provides completely confident that the Holy Spirit will equip them with leadership traits that will enable them to do the work that God has ordained for them. These traits of integrity, a positive attitude, ability to focus on goals, self-discipline, competencies, accountability and responsibility define Leadership Character.

Additionally, these same leadership traits enable a leader to be able to follow   other leaders with loyalty, dedication and enthusiasm. Therefore, the fundamental issue for a leader is being prepared morally, spiritually and professionally to serve in whatever capacity that the Holy Spirit directs. Beings mindful that the example that the leader demonstrates is continuously being observed and any negative actions or attitudes can have serious adverse, unintended consequences on the observer or observers, their lives and future. Therefore, along with the privilege that a leader has to lead and influence others to accomplish tasks and goals, the leader is equally responsible and accountable to ensure that his/her leadership efforts meet the test of treating other the way that he/she would like to be treated. "Proverbs 3:5-6 provide direction and confidence to achieve leadership excellence".

For Reflection...

> *"Leadership character development begins with
> the leader's willingness to accept the need for change."*
> —Larita M. Hand

THE HEART OF LEADERSHIP CHARACTER
Phil Kizzee
Associate Pastor, Northwest Church of the Nazarene

I suppose that in many circles today, the words "leadership" and "character" are not twins...or even bedfellows for that matter. This is a poor reflection on our society. For many, the idea of character has nothing to do with a person's ability to lead. In fact, someone who lives out what he or she believes, a person whose actions and words are synonymous with their values, is today seen as pious or even pompous. The Attorney General is being challenged for recent actions relating to physician-assisted suicide in Oregon. One writer was incensed that he, or anyone with leadership duties for that matter, "would allow their beliefs to influence their decisions" on such a matter. Have we really gone that far? Is anyone with a moral compass, no matter which way it may be pointed, supposed to lay it aside in order to be heard, followed or accepted in our society?

I believe that the words "leadership" and "character" are inseparable. A person without character may have the ability to lead, but it is leadership from the head. I choose to follow those who lead from the heart...and that kind of leadership flows from a heart of character first and wisdom second.

The heart of leadership character is formed with at least three ingredients: integrity, honesty and action.

Integrity: Character built on integrity is evident when a person's actions are parallel with their words and their words are aligned with their beliefs. Who I say I am must be who I am when no one is watching *and* when everyone is watching.

Honesty: This synergy of who a person is personally, privately and publicly is based on knowing oneself and being honest with what they know to be true about who they are. Anyone with public skills can pull off a "persona" but a person with character has an honest awareness of who they are and their life is consistent with this assessment. Character is not superficial, but is grounded in a deep, settled peace with who we really are.

Action: Character is an active ingredient in what it takes to be an authentic person. A person's character compels them to act when action is called for. Beliefs and standards are not calls to opinions, rather they are calls to action, and they demand a response. A person of character is also active in their pursuit of who they are now and who they are becoming.

Character and leadership may be separate topics for some, but true leadership is accomplished with spirit as well as skill. And spiritual leadership is based on being a person of character first and a leader second. There are many examples to be found in all realms of life and history. Personally, the model that Jesus of Nazareth gave to us is one that brings together perfectly the concepts of character and leadership. His words and actions flowed directly from His understanding of who he was and what he was here to accomplish. He was *painfully* honest with himself and others. His actions disturbed the status-quo on both sides of the issues of the day. And being true to who he was, his character demanded that he follow through with his words and beliefs and it sent him to the cross. Jesus accomplished his purpose, his life mission, while displaying for us the perfect blending of character and leadership.

When anyone separates character from personal actions, their influence is shattered. And since leadership is influence, a true leader is not only followed by his character, his character goes before him, making or breaking his ability to truly lead others.

121

> *"It is vital for leaders to remember that God
> desires to develop their character but they have to be
> willing, trusting, and obedient to His craftsmanship."*
> —Timothy A. Williams

THE HEART OF LEADERSHIP CHARACTER
Mike Little
District Supervisior, State Farm Insurance

The desire of an authentic leader is to energize, engage, and motivate others so worthy goals are achieved. This ability to translate vision into reality results when leaders value the potential of others and create an environment that inspires others to pursue their full potential.

Four things are crucial to being an effective leader: having strong character, being competent in areas of one's responsibilities, caring about others, and having the courage to take action and make decisions based on a sound moral foundation. In isolation, these leadership abilities will not necessarily make an effective leader. Rather, it is the blending of all four within the leader that promotes and encourages others to want to follow.

First, strong character in a leader lets others know what the leader demands for self (himself/herself) and others: to be trustworthy and honest. Strong character in a leader builds trust from others and provides a security and pride in the mission of the unit.

Secondly, competence in a leader lets others know that the leader "walks their talk." Leaders do not have to be an expert in all areas, but must have an awareness of their individual strengths and weaknesses and a strong desire to improve. Competence also builds on skills of wise recruitment and responsible delegation. This characteristic lets everyone know that each associate is a student who is expected to ask questions, seek answers, and improve their knowledge and competence base. Leaders expect everyone within the organization to move the mission forward.

Next, leaders know that all people have a strong desire to be appreciated and therefore they look for ways to make positive contributions to another person's life. Genuine caring expressed by leaders to others multiplies the leaders effectiveness. Leaders know that genuine caring validates expertise; "people don't care what you know until they know that you care." Strong leaders get to know their people, have a real concern for their lives and look for ways to encourage and support others in their life's journey.

Finally, courage in a leader is vital if the person is to be distinguished as an authentic leader. Courage is involved in day to day decisions that the leader must make. Courage to share the leader's heart. Courage to ask the hard question and make a difficult statement. Courage to say no. Courage to praise. Courage to be quiet and listen. Courage to confront others when they have compromised the mission. Courage to expect the best. Courage to admit when the leader has made a mistake of judgment or attitude. Courage to ask for help. Courage to do what's right when no one else is looking or when everyone else is compromising. Courage from dramatic challenges is built up by taking courage in the day to day events.

Leaders that stand on these four cornerstones of leadership are authentic leaders who have the potential to make an incredible positive impact on the lives of others and in the process accomplish sound goals and missions. Leaders know that the art of leadership is more about being on a journey than arriving at a destination and for that reason are constantly looking for ways to improve their ability to positively influence others.

For Reflection...
"Leadership is a rich and gracious gift from God. The sense of responsibility I feel as a leader, and the principles I cherish or espouse in relationship to this role, have been instilled by the Holy Spirit, as they are truly written on my heart, and, I think have been as long as I've recognized the calling of leadership."
—Jayne Cooper

THE HEART OF LEADERSHIP CHARACTER
C. Jay Matthews
Senior Pastor, Mt. Sinai Baptist Church

The past twenty-one years I have had the privilege of serving in ministry. The past thirteen years in pastoral ministry in the same church. I believe based upon my experience, the round table discussion and the presenters that character is the one element that can determine the success or failure of a leader in ministry. The character of a leader is the most important manifestation of the leaders relationship with Jesus Christ. It is the transforming power of God in the life of a leader that allows the leader to lead with integrity. It is important for leaders today as they look at developing specific skill sets that they understand the value of character.

The attributes in a leader that define character are important aspects of creating an atmosphere to process God's vision. It is the integrity, strength, courage, flexibility, wisdom, and honesty that allows a leader to fulfill the purpose that God has given him. One of the strengths of character is discovering God's purpose and then pursuing it with all diligence. To influence people for the purposes of God is a great responsibility. Leaders understand the need for accountability when they have strong character. Men and Women of God who lead the people of God with integrity develop people who do what the leader wants done with joy. Leaders who build strong relationships create an opportunity for transformation from what God is doing in their lives to what He wants to do in the lives of others.

Dr. John Stanko in his book, "So many leaders, so little leadership" says: "In the game Simon says, everyone tries to become Simon, the leader. But in real life, leading others is much more complex—its part preparation, part perspiration, and part inspiration." There are values that people respond to, that allows leaders to help the people of God find their purpose in Christ. The effective leader is one who allows the experience of Christ to become so real in their life that others will desire it for themselves.

We need leaders who impact others to change the way the world is. Phil Pringle in his book "You The Leader" says: "A leader is a cultural engineer. A value designer; leaders change the direction we're going. They take us higher. ...People who lead well, take us beyond where we would go if left to ourselves." It is important for leaders to develop a set of core values that transcend the current value system of the world. Those values such as: honesty, truthfulness, being compassionate, faithfulness, all have the potential to recreate those values in others.

Leaders must understand the power of vision and the need to be flexible with purpose. Vision allows leaders to see beyond the current dilemma of mankind, and to move people into directions that will create opportunities for God to change the circumstances, behaviors that keep men in their current predicament. Leaders with strong character become more than change agents, they can create change agencies, because of their development of teams of people who are change agents. The church of the Living God is in a pivotal position today to mentor and do role modeling around solid character values that people in the Body are in search of.

The two most important traits in a leaders life are: Competency and Character. Competency is what a leader does, and character is who the leader is. Therefore, a leader must be innovative, a team builder, a decision maker, have the ability to manage conflict, committed to a vision or purpose, and humane to others. These are the kind of traits that go beyond one's ability and reach deep down into the heart of who a person is. It is equally important today for leaders to have strong character as it is for them to be fully confident in their abilities.

For Reflection...
> *"A leader who is not authentic is no leader at all."*—George W. Cochran

THE HEART OF LEADERSHIP CHARACTER

Khushwant K. Pittenger
Professor of Business Administration
Chair of Undergraduate Business Program

A leader is characterized as someone who has followers. A great deal of writings on leadership, particularly in my area of expertise-- business management, focuses on the nature of relationship between a leader and his followers from a utilitarian point of view. This perspective is not unique to businesses. Effective leaders are considered to be those who can articulate their organizations' goals to their followers in a way that the followers embrace those goals as their own even at the cost of serious hardships. Transformational leadership and servant leadership are now frequently used terms in the leadership literature but that seemed not to have changed the underlying message of getting others to willingly do for the organization what the leader needs them to do regardless of the sacrifices. As I have approached mid-life and mid-career point, I have been distressed by my realizations.

The Sandbag Leadership Center's Round Table Convocation on Leadership Character on October 26 was a confirmation for me that I am not alone in my distress and business as a discipline, is not an anomaly in this regard. Religious organizations need to do as much soul searching as traditional business organizations. And deep, meaningful soul searching is needed by all leaders – not about how to increase the number of their followers or about how to convince others to make sacrifices for certain goals but about who they are and what is important to them and why.

A leader's character is the heart of leadership. But, what is character? Character is who you are; not what others think you are or what you want others to think you are or what you are in public or in private but who you are in your entirety. How many of us, when we are being brutally truthful, know who we are? Or are we truly who we think we are? At this convocation, I was fortunate enough to share the round table with participants who were courageous enough to share their struggle with their own personal "self-discovery." Getting to know one's true self is a noble goal but it is a hard journey. I am heartened to know that I am not alone in this struggle.

Bill Perkins advocated that a leader's character is the foundation on which a leader's accomplishments should be built. In other words, productive relationships with followers leading to distinction for the leader are desirable only when the leader is driven by ethics and values. Dr. Lovett Weems made a persuasive argument for leaders to build trust with their followers while Dr. Brown championed the cause of checks and balances in a system to protect the integrity of the honest.

These were all very inspirational messages and very engaging for the mind. In my mind, however, they ran the risk of becoming utilitarian. Are trust, ethics and moral values important because they help leaders sell others on their goals or are they important in their own right? No doubt, Bill, Lovett and Valerie would argue for the latter and agree with Paul Blease's message that we all have a unique mission in life. Our challenge is to figure out what it is and to stay true to it regardless of the difficulties and distractions. As Bill Blease very poignantly and metaphorically stated, "you don't want to climb a ladder to only find out that it is leaning against the wrong wall." The most daunting challenge for each one of us in life is not to climb a wall, no matter how steep or high, but to figure of which wall to climb and why. That has been my journey in the recent years and I hope it is your journey as well. Happy traveling my fellow travelers and God speed!

For Reflection...
> *"My prayer is that I do not rise to a place where my competencies supercede my character."*
> —Patricia Foote

THE HEART OF LEADERSHIP CHARACTER
Rick Ryding
Professor of Christian Education
Mt. Vernon Nazarene College

The heart of Christian leadership is personal authenticity. It begins with the death of the false self and the birth of the true self through transformation. Gone are the illusions that held the false self bound. A new freedom enables the leader, who is authentic, to create an environment where others can also be transformed, experience koinonia, and serve effectively.

Personal authenticity is a prerequisite to servant leadership. Only someone who is free can create a spacious place for people to gather and be themselves. Conventional wisdom would suggest that this is risky because organizations need their personnel to be predictable in order to produce a consistent product. At some point Christian organizations must become communities where persons have the freedom to **be**: to tell their story, to trust, to communicate openly, to celebrate their diversity, to create, to become effective. Such a community is born in the spacious heart of a leader who has made the transformative inward journey. First inward...

127

A Christian organization does not simply exist to fulfill an external mission, but to first embrace an internal mission: to build community, to nurture the lives of their employees into Christlikeness, and the discovery of their true selves. In many organizations, folks must create, and live behind, the mask of a false self in order to keep up appearance or measure up to an external standard. There is a deeper calling. It is to enable others to discover their true selves and, out of that awareness, to live authentically. This requires a leader who has made the difficult journey into the depths of their own soul, and can guide others on their journey. Parker Palmer said, "Good leadership comes from people who have penetrated their own inner darkness and arrived at the place where we are at one with one another, people who can lead the rest of us to the place of 'hidden wholeness' because they have been there and know the way." (Palmer, Let your life speak, 80-81) A leader gives others the ability to enter their inner reality and navigate it to self-acceptance, personal wholeness, and then "our complex and inexplicable caring for each other." (Palmer citing Annie Dillar, 82.)...then outward.

The spacious heartedness of the leader is the catalyst for effective growth in grace, personal maturity, and authenticity of the organization's personnel. Such leadership creates a healthy organizational culture in which respect, collegiality, collaboration and creativity are catalyzed. Visions and ministries are born out of the communities shared life together. Ownership becomes the norm; effective service the outcome.

The heart of servant leadership is personal authenticity. It invites people to be themselves, to be grace to one another, and unique participants in the community, and creators of its mission and vision.

THE HEART OF LEADERSHIP CHARACTER
Bev Spreng
Executive Director of Leadership Ashland
Community Volunteer Extraordinaire

Heart is defined by Webster as *the most important and/or central part of something.* At the *heart* of leadership character lies all that the word *heart* encompasses. To *speak from the heart* means to speak with *deep sincerity.* To *take heart* means to *encourage.* To *set one's heart on* means to *desire very strongly.* To *wear one's heart on one's sleeve* means to *express one's feelings to the world.* To *have something at heart* is to *have great interest in.* To *have the heart to do*

128

something is to *have the courage to do something. With all one's heart-* most willingly.

Putting it all together: To lead you must have a passion for something; something you feel strongly about; something about which you are willing to express your feelings to the world; something you sincerely care about and have great interest in; something you have the courage and the willingness to act on, to do something about, and something you can sincerely encourage others to believe in.

To lead one must care enough and be courageous enough to risk. To risk, one must have faith; faith in one's self, faith in convictions, faith in others to follow and help, faith in God's presence and support. Faith gives us the confidence to act and gives hope to our passion. So we have heart - a combination of faith, passion, courage. All necessary to the motivation to take the lead, but not sufficient to take the lead. We must couple the heart with energy, with action. Just as our hearts would be still without blood to rush through them, our faith, passion and courage (our *heart)* would be for naught if we had not the energy to take action, to make vital our vision. Just as our passion, faith and courage stimulates the energy to act, our actions give life to our passions and visions. They are interdependent. Our strength within is reflected externally in the strength and energy of our actions.

Does this mean that leaders need to do it all themselves? Are leaders required to be the visionaries and the doers? Another component to successful leadership, which allows an individual to function most effectively and efficiently, is awareness and respect of ones strengths and weaknesses coupled with an awareness and respect of the strengths of others. As mentioned earlier in this writing, to lead, one must believe strongly enough to be able to encourage others to believe as well. When others believe as strongly as you, then your strengths and your energies can combine to achieve a common goal. An efficient and effective leader combines his heart and his energy with the heart and energy of others, drawing from his talents and the talents of others to fulfill a common vision.

To lead, one must have the *heart* to lead and the *heart* to encourage the *heart* of others. This may mean, at times, stepping aside and letting others "take the lead". For instance, perhaps one has a marvelous vision, the heart (passion, courage, faith) and the energy to fulfill the vision but perhaps not the skill or the means required. By encouraging the heart of someone with the appropriate skills and/or means, and allowing them to share your vision, allowing them to lead as

129

well, you move forward towards your goal with a combined energy and even better chances of seeing your vision through to reality. This could be difficult if your motives are egocentric, if it's all about power and recognition. But if it's about achieving a goal, empowering others, and working as a team, then encouraging the heart of others should not be a problem.

Heart (passion, courage, faith)**,** *energy/action, encouraging/empowering others***.** Effective leadership happens when all three combine, where all three intersect. There lies the heart of leadership character.

For Reflection...
   "As my Heavenly Father equips and cultivates leadership characteristics in me, may I wear this costume to gently share the most enduring, consistent, passionate drama man can experience. The most important less I take away today is that I am worthy in God's sight."—Holly Finks

Learning Exercise #15: Uncovering Your Ideal Self

Read the nine essays on "The Heart of Leadership" in this chapter. Each expresses a personal search for that ideal self.

Read the stories reflectively. To do so, ask yourself these questions as you are reading:

- What thoughts are coming into my mind as I read? – Jot them down.

- What biblical passages does this bring to my mind? – Jot them down.

- What questions or difficulties do I see in applying this? – Jot them down.

- Where does this ring true with my experience? – Jot them down.

- How might this apply to my life/my leadership? – Jot them down.

Write a vision for yourself and your leadership. Describe the leader you want to become. Describe the core principles or values that you will hold.

Describe a day in the future when you have become the leader you want to be.

Choose a date six to nine years in the future. Imagine you are the leader you want to become. Describe a day in your life. Use as many details as possible.

Share your vision with trusted friends. Choose two or three trusted individuals to share your vision and your imaginary day in the future. Ask your friends to help you by answering two questions:

- Is there anything about my ideal self that you already see in my life today? (These are strengths you will want to build on.)

- What are two or three things I could begin to do now that would help me become the leader I want to be? (Consider these suggestions as you write your action plan.)

Chapter 6
The Daily Challenge:
Character Counts with Every Step

Every leader experiences moments when leadership responsibilities conflict with personal values. Cutbacks force them to choose between reducing services to clients or laying off a loyal employee. Unexpected demands force a choice between attending a son's ballgame or meeting a major donor who has unexpectedly arrived from out of town. Such choices are between two right things. No matter what you choose, you feel short-changed.

In these situations, leaders follow a variety of paths. Some think about what an admired mentor might do. Others talk it over with trusted friends and family. Still others go with their "gut instinct." These decisions come in the everyday routines as well as unexpected challenges. They become the path of character development.

In this chapter, you will read how five leaders deal with moments that demand character. These demanding moments are:

1. Moments that Define
2. Moments of Discontinuity
3. Moments of Tension
4. Moments of Reflection
5. Moments of Community

Moments That Define

Joseph L. Badaracco, Jr., in his book *Defining Moments: When Managers Must Choose Between Right and Right*, says that these moments form, reveal, and test our character. Character is formed because a leader commits to an irreversible course of action that will impact your identity. These moments reveal something about the leader that may have only been partially known. These moments test leaders because they have to live up to personal ideals. In the article that follows, Paul Sears describes a "defining moment" in his leadership of the School of Business at Ashland University.

For Reflection...
> *"Critical to my leadership abilities will be the persistent act of developing, right now, what I will value most at the end of my life."*—Jeff Branche

LEADERSHIP CHARACTER MAKES THE DIFFERENCE IN MY WORK
Paul Sears
Dean, School of Business
Ashland University

If the learned pattern of effective behavior that defines leadership character must encompass both external and internal change efforts (see my paper on Strengths and Crisis of Leadership Character), then how does one learn to do this? There is still controversy in the leadership studies area as to whether leadership behavior can be taught. Clearly leadership principles can be taught, but can those principles be made tacit and translated into consistently effective *behaviors*?

Many would say "yes". The armed forces, for one. The various branches of the armed forces have invested enormous amounts of resources in creating systems for making officers and leaders out of a significant portion of their recruits. While the military would not argue that everyone can be turned into a leader, they would probably agree that a willing and able recruit with the requisite mental and physical skills can be transformed into a leader through their leadership training and development efforts. Indeed, they regularly bet millions of dollars and even the lives of service people on their ability to do just that.

As the Dean of a collegiate business school, I would bet that schools, colleges, universities and seminaries would probably hedge their answers more than the military. While many of these institutions boast mission statements that claim they create leaders, in fact the primarily educational outcomes on which they focus attention and resources rarely include leadership behaviors per se. While undoubtedly some students at these institutions do develop effective leadership behaviors (for which the schools then try to take credit), these outcomes are not as intentional and predictable as the educational institutions would like to suggest they are.

Finally, many would argue that leadership (particularly the charismatic or transformative form of leadership behavior) cannot be taught but is largely innate, or at least cannot be predictably developed and enhanced by our existing methods of leadership development. But all of these arguments focus on leadership behavior that is primarily external in its focus. Little attention is paid to the notion of leadership or change management with an internal focus.

Except the church almost all religions have a "messenger from God" model leader who not only attempts to change the external world and influence people in that world, but who also goes through and models a transformative internal change. Thus the world's religions seem to model the ideal and most effective form of leadership character which is focused on both external and internal change and transformation. This is the strength of leadership character as developed through religious study and vicarious learning.

Leadership character as developed through religious and pastoral study and vicarious learning that defines the "religious approach" to leadership character enjoys only a peripheral role in the scholarly dialogue on leadership. One thread of the leadership dialogue that bridges the secular and religious approaches to leadership is that of "servant leadership". Servant leadership has developed, in part, through a study of Jesus and his leadership style. However, there is also a conscious, even self-conscious, attempt to make servant leadership a secular model of leadership character. Given the strengths of

135

approaching leadership through the study of religion, with its balanced focus on both external and internal change management, it may be time for the religious approach to assert itself into the dialogue on leadership more insistently, especially in light of some of the recent and more dramatic examples of the failure of the secular leadership model at the highest levels of government.

However, business school faculty are often reluctant to employ an approach that combines deep, personal, transformative change with traditional leadership studies. I am not referring to the superficial personal style adjustments suggested by the situational leadership literature, but rather developing a profound sense of personal and organizational mission and vision linked to a unique organizational context and expressing itself in behaviors that are apt and effective in that particular organizational culture.

There are several reasons why business school faculty are reluctant to go down this path. One reason is that most faculty were not trained in a religious or personally transformative context. Their lack of training and perspective on the importance of personal change accounts for a significant part of the disconnect between personal change in leaders and successful organizational change.

But I think business school faculty may hesitate to focus on the importance of personal transformation in part because they are afraid to loose their "expert" status. As content experts, the theories, models and frameworks of the leadership literature provide unending opportunities to demonstrate their expertise. But personal transformation is not a subject that they can easily demonstrate their superiority over their students. Indeed, some of the students may be experiencing college as a personal transformation and possess more experiential data on the subject than their professors.

Finally, faculty seems to be reluctant to prescribe answers or solutions for students, preferring that the student find their own answers. Theories and concepts permit students to do that, but requiring them to change seems too prescriptive. However, some schools are beginning to recognize that the business world is suggesting, even demanding, change. As more and more business schools adopt an "outcomes-oriented, continuous-improvement approach" to accreditation, they are being encouraged to define outcomes in terms that are important to key stakeholders in their environment. And for business schools, the employers and other key players in the business world are obviously key stakeholders.

What these stakeholders are making clear is that integrity and honesty are important student outcomes. As business schools listen more carefully to their key stakeholders, they are being forced to become more prescriptive. Businesses want graduates who possess integrity. Followers want leaders who have integrity. Business school faculty are beginning to respond with information and courses like "Business Ethics". Some schools are even going beyond the expectation that students must know about ethics, to the notion that students must practice ethical behavior.

The concept of leadership character provides a foundation for my own efforts to encourage our faculty to adopt integrity and accountability as competencies in our outcomes-assessment model. We have not reached consensus on this issue yet, but we are moving in the right direction.

For Reflection...
"The role of the leader is to courageously orchestrate opposing dynamics so that his followers can become the fulfillment of their calling"—Doug Cooper

Moments of Discontinuity

Richard Boyatzis speaks of leadership development in terms of discoveries that are discontinuous. By that he means they are moments when we catch a glimpse of our ideal self and/or real self in such a clear and forceful way that we can no longer settle for business as usual. Such moments of discontinuity are opportunities to examine values, patterns, decisions, and behavior. They are moments that create motivation for change. Thus, they are moments of character development. In the

137

following article, LeBron Fairbanks describes a moment of discontinuity during a presentation on the continent of Africa.

LEADERSHIP CHARACTER MAKES THE DIFFERENCE IN MY
WORK
E. LeBron Fairbanks
President, Mt. Vernon Nazarene College

"Two are better than one, because they have a good reward for their toil. For if they fail, and one falls, one will lift up the other; but woe to one who is alone and falls and does not have another to help...two will withstand...a three-fold cord is not quickly broken." Ecclesiastes 4:9-12

A few months ago, I had the privilege of speaking to a group of Church of the Nazarene educators in Johannesburg, South Africa. The setting was the first Consultation on Global Faculty Development for the denomination. Nazarene educators, particularly from the two-thirds world spent a week together probing the possibilities of an Academy for International Education in the Church of the Nazarene. My part in the conference program was to lead two sessions on the subject of institutional collaboration. The title of my presentations was "Institutional Collaboration as Academy Strategy." I addressed the need for intra- and inter-institutional strategy as foundational for the denomination to "maximize access" to the rich resources of the educational institutional institutions of the Church of the Nazarene worldwide, particularly in the two-thirds world.

It was a wonderful experience for me. I met many friends from around the world. However, something happened to me while I was there. My purpose was to assist other educators. Instead I found myself asking some hard questions about my leadership character at MVNC, and the degree to which I model the partnership and collaboration I "preach" at the institution I serve. I was asking probing questions about my personal integrity. Was the strategic process I was thought I was championing at MVNC falling on deft ears? If so, why?

I returned to the MVNC campus determined to share with the faculty and staff my "moment of truth," to outline some specific steps for us to take together, and to request for the campus community to hold me accountable to my word. If "trust is the foundation of effective leadership" (Weens), then I must be the change I seek to produce in the MVNC faculty and staff before institutional collaboration is to become a way of life on our campus.

Let me summarize what I said to the educators in Johannesburg, and then identify some questions I asked the MVNC faculty and staff about our relationships.

I re-emphasized to the conference participants that "leadership rises up at the intersection of personal passion and public need." I suggested that every organization needs a "champion" for the collaborative process, if partnering or collaborating is to become a way of life for an institution, and not just an intellectual game. I presented some lessons learned at MVNC about collaboration.

- Using collaboration to manage change is challenging.
- A vision and need are required for success.
- Regular communications is the glue of collaboration.
- Active, committed leadership at the senior administrative level and an informed and broad-based steering committee are required.
- The greater the trust and communication, the faster and more profound is the benefit.
- Institutional collaboration must become institutional strategy.

Using Winer's model, I asked the participants to evaluate their institutions regarding the following factors with ratings of high, medium, or low, even as I participated in the process by evaluating MVNC regarding successful collaborative efforts:

Environment: History and leadership? Favorable climate?

Membership: Trust? In member's self interest? Able to compromise?

Structure: Flexible? Clear Roles and Guidelines?

Communication: Open and frequent? Established links?

Purpose: Attainable Goals? Shared vision?

Resources: Sufficient Funds? Sufficient Time? Skilled Facilitator?

139

Before I completed the presentation, I made some remarks using quotes I had included for them in a booklet I had distributed. But as I was speaking to THEM, I found myself speaking to myself as the MVNC. I sincerely want to increase the level of involvement and trust between the administration and the campus community of employees. The power of three (or more) as affirmed in the Ecclesiastes is a powerful image and necessary concept for an institution seeking to make embrace collaboration as strategy.

Indeed, institutional collaboration must become institutional strategy at MVNC. This is my passion. But it will not happen simply by the institutional president making pronouncements. It will happen if we within the academic community passionately believe with Helen Keller that "alone we can do so little, together we can do so much."

More specifically, I returned to MVNC and shared with the campus community the following commitments:

- I want to affirm each of you as brothers and sisters in Christ whom I choose work at MVNC as a vocational calling.

- With this affirmation will come a renewed emphasis on continued training and development. The staff development committee is being restructured and will provide ongoing staff development throughout the year

- I will work closely with a task force specifically and with the campus community during next eighteen months to streamline the administrative and decision making structures. The goal is to facilitate, not inhibit, you in accomplishing your vocational assignments and realizing your ministry goals at MVNC. "None of us is as smart as all of us."

- I ask for your assistance in revising the document, FOR THIS WE STAND: VALUES UNDERLYING THE MVNC FAITH COMMUNITY. I wrote this document in 1993 with your feedback when I realized that MVNC was enrolling an increasing number of students with no previous connection to MVNC or understanding to the sponsoring denomination of the institution. I again need you counsel. I need to work with me in revising the important document.

- The MVNC vision statement needs revising. I shared with the MVNC Board of Trustees recently that needed to revise the present MVNC statement. The cabinet has reviewed a draft revision statement formed by Chaplain Sivewright and his team. I want each of you to review and comment on the statement before a final revision is prepared for the Board of Trustees to approve.

- A task force has been working to revise the MVNC master campus development plan in light of enrollment growth projections for the next twenty years and the recent acquisition of the Pinecrest farm across Martinsburg Road. The campus now consists of 401 acres. You will have another opportunity to review the several scenarios developed by the task force and our consultants before recommendations are forwarded to the Board of Trustees for consideration.

- A Board appointed task force is studying the issue of university status for MVNC. The MVNC faculty and staff will have an opportunity to discuss the information and tentative recommendations already forwarded to you in the mail.

- I want to find ways to periodically update the campus community regarding our progress in developing an operating budget proposal for the Board of Trustees. I believe you trust us, but I think the budget planning committee can do a more effective job in communicating with you the process, progress, problems, and potential regarding the budget building experience.

I shared with the campus community the African proverb that states, *"When the elephant fights, it is the grass that suffers."* (Proverb of the Kikuyu people of Africa)

The proverb means that when the people in power (the leaders) fight, it is the "grass-roots" people who get hurt." I seek to empower and support the faculty and staff. Yet I wonder if the structure presently in place facilitates or inhibits the "grass roots" of this institution from working and relating at their peak potential.

I concluded my remarks to the faculty and staff by stating, "In a new and profound way since my Johannesburg experience, to a degree I don't think has characterized me in the past, I want to understand,

141

embrace, and lead the academic faith community at MVNC from the perspective reflected in the eight commitments outlined above."

Integrity. Character. Vulnerability. Community. Courage. Conviction. Gratitude. Hope Trust. These words shape an institutional leader of an academic faith community who seeks to lead from a Christian value base. Have I succeeded in all that was outlined above to the MVNC faculty and staff? No! Interestingly, more was accomplished that one might expect. The issue, however, is not so much a "checklist" of accomplishments as the growth of the leader in both competence and character. And the growth of the led!

Since the event on campus when I presented the above material to the faculty and staff, I have continued to think about the broader theme of leadership character, particularly as the imperative relates to leading an academic community of faith in the midst of diverse personalities, conflicting expectations, differing faith traditions, distinct assignments and various levels of maturity. Leadership character becomes the issue for the leader. Character counts—big time!

Leadership character is the connection between "The Power of Three (or more)" and institutional collaboration. For institutional collaboration to become institutional strategy in an academic faith community, a spirituality of leadership must be forged and embraced. I seek to lead and learn from this perspective and commitment.

"May it be so Lord for me and the people with whom I serve." Amen.

Moments of Tension

Moments of character formation "force us to find a balance between our hearts in all their idealism and our jobs in all their messy reality" (Badaracco, *Defining Moments*). Such a moment is not a mere intellectual exercise. This is an opportunity to examine ideals, sharpen vision, cultivate creative strategies, and stretch us into personal growth. In the next article, Mary Kaufmann allows us to see the personal tension of her everyday work assignment.

142

LEADERSHIP CHARACTER MAKES THE DIFFERENCE IN MY WORK!
Mary Kaufmann
Director, Sales Development
Longaberger Company

Have you ever stopped to ask yourself what is the purpose of your work? Most people would answer that the purpose of their work is "to make money to live." There are some that work because they find it enjoyable, but this is more the exception than the rule. Regardless of the purpose behind our work, it is obvious that work is a very real and necessary part of our life.

Webster's Dictionary defines work as "physical or mental effort or activity directed toward the production or accomplishment of something."[1] Simply put, **work is about making progress**. We look at our current state and see that our circumstances have room for improvement. An endless list of steps exist to grow, fix and prepare for a better tomorrow. The attributes of work seem full of promise but to what end? We keep growing and getting better for the next snapshot in time from which to make the next set of improvements. If the human race could rise high above this regular routine of improvements, as if to observe from outside itself, we might find it silly or meaningless just as we laugh at a dog chasing its tail.

How can we find real purpose and a deep sense of accomplishment in our routine of making progress and improvements? How do we find meaning in our daily work no matter what the task? If the goal is narrowly defined as "to make progress" we must add a special ingredient to the mix, as in a recipe, in order to bake "purpose and meaning" into the end result. This ingredient has nothing to do with how competent or skilled we are at the tasks we perform in our work, it has everything to do with the method and manner by which we approach our work. The powerful ingredient we must add to our approach is a heaping spoonful of the desire to serve others rather than to serve ourselves. **Serving others is the cornerstone of strong leadership character in our work.**

Think about the past several years of your work life. What are the experiences and accomplishments that have touched you as being meaningful and worthwhile? We are likely to forget the details of a project or deadline but will highly regard the people who supported us along the way. When we receive rave reviews and recognition, we may feel wonderful and 'high on life' for a brief period. However, over time,

143

the only feelings that last are those that are tied to the relationships we build on our journey for progress.

What prevents us from focusing on the most important elements that leave lasting impressions for the greater good? Why do we forget to care about and build relationships with the people around us as we climb the ladder of success? Why are we so self-centered? Within every human is the desire for acceptance, praise and love whether we will admit it or not. The desire for acceptance is arguably one of the deeply rooted of all desires. When we are faced with the need for quick action among the thousands of decisions we make every day, usually our most deeply rooted desire will take control over our actions. If we **care more about being recognized** than we **care about others** then our actions over time will result in "working without a purpose." We will be spending our life wasting time chasing our tail and expending our energy with no real value or meaning to show for our work.

How do we create an environment where people would rather serve others than serve themselves? How do we move from being a leader who cares more about being recognized to one who cares more about the recognition of others? I would suggest the following roadmap as a way to become a servant leader.

Step 1. Look within Yourself. Why should you care about serving others? Why be motivated to do good for others? There are two perspectives from which to approach finding the answers to these questions, one has to do with the benefits to us while here in this life, the other relates to our eternal life after death.

We have all heard the expression that states "when we do 'good' for others it comes back to us ten-fold." When I offered an expression of kindness and caring to someone it came back to me in an amazing way. Some years ago while at work I was on the phone helping a customer with an issue. I took just a little extra time to help her with her problem. Through our conversation I learned that she was very ill and battling breast cancer. For weeks, I couldn't stop thinking of this woman, her three children and her battle for life. So my daughter and I would remember her and her family in our prayers.

Fast forward several months later and a gentleman was hired as a new employee at my company. To make a long story short I was astonished to learn that he was the husband of the woman I had been praying for. You see, he came to find me and introduce himself, he wanted to thank me for making such a difference to his wife. He was hired into a position of authority and invited me to join his team. He offered me a promotion and an opportunity to be involved with work that was exciting and of great interest to me. I could hardly believe God blessed me in this way!

What about the benefits from our goodness in life after death? In Matthew 6:19-21 it states,

> *"Do not store up for yourselves treasure on earth, where moth and rust destroy, and where thieves break in and steal. But store up for yourselves treasures in heaven, where moth and rust do not destroy, and where thieves do not break in and steal. For where your treasure is, there your heart will be also."[2]*

In a few words this scripture is saying, "good things come to those who wait." We cannot, in our wildest imagination, understand what wonders await us in heaven. I have felt God's blessings here on earth in many of the simple pleasures of life; the laughter from the bellies of my children, the quenching taste of cool water on a hot day and so much more. Compared to these, Heaven will be awesome in its blessings. Why not work toward the unimaginable treasures in heaven. The Bible tells us it will surely be worth the wait.

Step 2. Find a good role model. The best role model in the history of the world was Jesus Christ. Who was Jesus? He was a man who lived a real life, died a painful death for our sins and was astonishingly resurrected to give us everlasting life. Aside from his Godliness, he was humble, kind, forgiving, and so much more.

We spend our lives in pursuit of being the best, coming in first, and fighting our way to the top. He was very clear about his thoughts on putting ourselves first. In Mark 9:25, Jesus says, "If anyone wants to be first, he must be the very last, and the servant of all."[3] Compare yourself to Him. Ask the tough questions of your character and actions toward others. Ask others for honest feedback. Assess your past for the opportunities you missed to help someone else because you were too busy helping yourself. You'll figure out if you are self-centered in your style if you notice a pattern of behavior that puts you first. I have to admit I noticed this behavior about myself.

There are many ways in which I could describe the self-centeredness of my past. One example is that when I would be in a group I found myself doing most of the talking. I didn't like silence so I felt more comfortable to just keep right on talking. When I studied Jesus' life, his character and his service to others I could easily see my self-centeredness. It was hard to face this fact about myself but once I realized the truth it didn't take long to change and it feels so good let other people talk.

I was recently on a business trip with a group of ten people who work together. I barely said anything the entire evening, except to go around the table and ask each of them to tell their story. They spent three hours sharing, laughing and reminiscing. After that evening I received notes from three of the people who were there, telling me how wonderful I was. They shared words of thanks and said how good it was get to know me, when my quiet contribution of the evening was simply to listen. When I look back on that evening and remember their faces, they were shining. In the warmth of their glow was a wonderful place to be. I would not have had the pleasure of getting to know these people if I had not studied the life of Jesus and begun to follow His lead.

Step 3. Gain acceptance and love from God. As I mentioned before, we all want to be accepted, to be part of the crowd, and to be recognized. When we make a habit of wanting acceptance, more than wanting to be helpful, we have a problem. The answer is easy; we can have an abundance of acceptance, love and attention from the greatest man to ever walk the Earth. When we accept Jesus into our life, he gives us everything we need to feel good about our life and ourselves. When we feel this peace deep in the center of our soul we begin to want to do more for others than we do for ourselves.

Personally, when I accepted Jesus into my life and began my life journey with Him, I was transformed in my relating to others. I can remember the stress of sitting in meetings with people who were making wrong assumptions about the work of my team. They did not have all the facts nor did they seem interested in the entire picture of the situation. I would find myself struggling with questions of how to give them the full picture without appearing defensive. Even when I spoke up I always wondered later if my actions had helped or hurt the outcome.

Today my actions are different, besides placing Jesus squarely seated at the table in my prayers during the meeting, I imagine His support, acceptance and understanding of my side of the story even when I sense that no one else cares about it. I care **less about what others think** about me and **more about what Jesus thinks** of me. We get all the recognition and praise we need from Jesus. His love fills us up and allows us to overflow with recognition and praise to others. When we

146

follow Him, we can't help but to have a deep desire to serve others. Service becomes a natural part of our life.

It is my firm belief that the best style of leadership is reflected in those leaders who desire to serve rather than to be served. They lead from the position of strength that comes from following Jesus. They get all the acceptance and recognition they need from God. Find your path into this type of leadership by molding your style to one who follows Jesus.

Reflect What You've Learned. Imagine looking into a very large mirror. The reflection causes you to see things exactly the opposite as they really are. I ask you to consider that the same effect occurs with the result of our work if we are not serving others. When our methods are without leadership character, we work very hard and end up with the exact opposite result we most deeply desire – to be accepted, loved and admired. When we work for our own self-interest, people see right through us and do not like what they see. In the other hand, when we work as a servant leader; people admire and respect our character. The cornerstone of leadership character, servant leadership, is demonstrated in the kind and gentle method of serving others throughout our daily routine of work. Look into the mirror and see yourself as the leader in whom God's image you were made, one who really cares.

NOTES

1. Anne H. Soukhanov, Webster's II New Riverside University Dictionary, (Boston, MA: Houghton Mifflin Company), 1327.
2. Kenneth Barker, *The NIV Study Bible* (Michigan: The Zondervan Corporation, 1985), 1452.
3. Ibid, 1512.

Moments of Reflection

Often, great lessons in character development come when you reflect on your journey. Such reflection entails learning from triumphs and regrets, applying guiding principles to new situations, and recognizing the patterns of behaving and relating that make you a good leader. In the next article, Rod Bushey shares the journey of his own leadership.

LEADERSHIP CHARACTER MAKES THE DIFFERENCE IN MY WORK!
Rod Bushey
High School Choral Director
Howell, Michigan

The underlying theme of leadership is based on the trust of those you lead. Building trust is a process that takes time that involves demonstrating a life of integrity in front and away from those you influence. This ultimately results in establishing credibility. Our trust is more readily accepted as we build healthy relationships within the structure. Credibility is therefore built one person at a time as we work to develop trust.

My greatest realm of influence involves work with teenagers in a high school choral music setting. There has been established, across the past 29 years, an infrastructure to serve as an extension of me to the students in each class. The need to develop this infrastructure resulted from a program that grew from one hundred sixty to over four hundred forty singers across the past fifteen years. The daily operation of conducting classes of sixty, eighty, or over one hundred students in a single class presents problems that cannot be solved by one person. Various student leaders in each choir class perform organizational duties that allow each choir to spend optimal time on rehearsal.

Sharing the Dream

The dream to create a program grew out of a desire for my students to be part a successful high school experience that will instill pride and self-esteem among the participants. It also was a priority to make the high school choir a place to belong in a school of over 2300 students and to experience a well rounded music education. This dream gave birth to a vision that has been shared at selected times with students, parents, community, and administration.

The development of trust was the forerunner of the shared vision. It was apparent that trust was something I would have to work at developing with the students. They need to time to process the shared vision and be free to communicate with the leadership. There were numerous hours spent talking with and, of course, listening to many students. It was, and is, my ultimate responsibility to shape the direction and philosophy of the program while giving my kids a voice in the process.

Point 'Em in the Right Direction

When I began my teaching career, someone said to me, "If you're working with high school kids, just point 'em in the right direction, and then get out of the way". That statement provided challenge and inspiration at the same time. Challenge, because I was not confident that I could give direction that they would understand. Challenge, because I hoped they could and would grasp my vision. The inspiration was based on a deep seated desire for my students to experience a level of success from the start.

Since my primary training was in instrumental music, moving into a choral music position as my first assignment created a determination to rise to a new challenge. One personality trait that has been characteristic of my teaching style is an openness and honesty in front of my classes. If I sensed a weakness in my understanding or ability, I would admit that to my class and proceed to devise ways to improve. I consulted with colleagues in other schools and sought the council of successful choral directors to help strengthen my approach to choral music instruction.

As a result, my transparency created a lack of confidence with some of my students who were gifted leaders. We produced a musical at the end of my first year. This group of leaders, a nucleus of young men, auditioned and received only minor roles. They decided be a part of the production, but from a distance. The previous choral director had a strong background in drama and I made it very clear my strength was music and not drama.

Consequently, there was more emphasis on choral music and less on drama. This group of young men made a consensus decision to let me produce the musical and limit their cooperation.

One staff member made a statement regarding my limited resource of experience stating: "...what you lacked in ability you made up for with enthusiasm". It became apparent that a positive and enthusiastic approach to a problem served to inspire confidence in the musical cast. Rehearsals progressed through performances and finally the closing night, marking the last performance of the year.

The aforementioned group of young men met asked to speak with me on stage following the show. Their response was a tremendous encouragement to this young teacher. They said, "We have not been very supportive this year. We wanted to stand back because we did not think you knew what you were doing. We are sorry and want to apologize for how we treated you. Please understand that we will be one hundred percent behind you next year and do whatever you want of us."

Needless to say, we had a very successful choir the following year and those young men became the leadership that was expected. Their positive attitude added a level of energy to the daily rehearsals and performances creating a cohesive spirit and overwhelming sense of pride.

Creating leadership in students begins by guiding attitudes that yield confidence from their peers. It becomes necessary to help those you lead to realize your vision. Leaders create the correct response when our motive to succeed is not selfish, but carries the best interest of those you lead. Only when you can impress students with the realization that your motive is for their success can you truly be a leader with trust from your constituents.

"Get Out of the Way"
This has been most rewarding aspect of creating a leadership model and character. When my students are released to lead, and are successful, then can I realize the level of learning that has taken place. There are numerous responsibilities assigned each student leader to make the choir activities run smoothly. Student leaders become an extension of myself. When performing the task at hand, they are modeling responsible behavior with the attitude that they must complete the job.

A few weeks ago, we were rehearsing for a concert to be held the following night. The choir president, elected by her peers, asked me if she could speak to the group. I simply stepped aside and she proceeded to talk to the group about their lack of rehearsal intensity the past few days. Her words were well chosen and received by the ensemble. The respect she receives and deserves is a direct result of her own work ethic demonstrated from day to day. Needless to say we had an excellent practice.

By her words, Leah, the choir president, put action to the statement "...just get out of the way". Examples, such as the one described above, are part of the daily routine by the elected officers. My role continues to be an encourager and guide the decisions of the entire choir council. The council is made up of the leadership in each of the five choirs that meet every day. Among their duties are: attendance taking; keeping fund raising records of each student; producing concert programs; planning social activities; making certain their ensemble has uniform needs met; and publicizing upcoming concerts or choir activities. The success of the program leans heavily on the responsible results of the choir officer's actions.

Character traits that need to be demonstrated in student leaders include responsibility, integrity, modeling behavior, and a servant attitude. When these qualities are evident among the leadership, the students who elected them gain confidence, pride, and desire to be enthusiastic members of the choir. These characteristics have made the idea of "...getting out of the way" a remarkable experience from this educator's point of view.

For Reflection...
> *"The concept that we have discussed at this conference that has had the most personal impact on me is "grace". I want to become more "grace-full." I want to become more "grace-full" so that, as a leader, I can share that grace with others."*—Paul Sears

Moments of Community

One of the abiding lessons of the Roundtable is that leaders need community. Specifically, leaders need a community of leaders. By listening, interacting, reflecting, challenging, restating, and bonding, leaders wrestle with conflicting values, behavior patterns, significant choices, and the quality of character that results from these discussions. Larita Hand describes her experience of character development through the Roundtable.

"LEADERSHIP CHARACTER MAKES THE DIFFERENCE IN MY WORK"
Larita Hand
Executive Director, Mercy Ministries

Leadership Character makes the difference in my work with families in crisis and mentoring leaders because the people I serve desire to know that the leader is competent and sustains a Godly character in all aspects of the leaders life. Therefore it is essential that I take time to develop my personal leadership character. The people I am serving are brokenhearted and bruised and need direction from some one that they can trust and believe that the leader has the capability to lead them with moral and ethical values.

Trust and Creditability were two competencies that a leader must develop when working with people in the church or businesses. In my work with leaders it is imperative that I develop a bond of trust with them through the mentoring process. In the mentoring process I state to the leader that I have bonded myself to a vow of confidentiality to enable the leader to know that they can build a trusting relationship with me and that I will attempt to be creditable as a leader.

The people I serve want to know that they can depend on me to be not only creditable for the organization but also in the community. I shared in the group session that I was faced with an issue of creditability with my organization. We used a hotel chain in my city for a conference and the hotel overdraft out of the organizations account without permission, which caused insufficient funds for all of our outstanding checks. It was my responsibility as the leader to rectify the problem. In light of the hotel's error they reimbursed the organization all of the funds. I learned from this experience patience and endurance through this issue of creditability, accountability and integrity.

In developing leadership character the mentoring relationship helps the mentee to find the purpose and meaning for their life. In my work with leaders, I challenge them to find their purpose in life and assist them in the search for meaning. The leader should have a vision, purpose and goals to fulfill the mission in his/her life. In my work I have to instill hope, vision and purpose in the lives of the brokenhearted and bruised. It is essential that the people I serve see me modeling behavior that demonstrates that I have vision and purposefully driven to obtain the goals for the organizations and the people we serve.

The greatest challenge in Leadership Character development is to maintain humility in the transformational process of becoming a Godly Leader in my personal life, church, business and the people I serve. In the last group session of the roundtable, the group members did a summation of their experiences. I began to identify that I had been transformed in my Leadership development through the process of information from the keynote speakers. Each of the speakers addressed the development of Leadership Character from their own personal frame of reference through their work ethic. The dialogue in the groups enables me to process how I respond as a leader in a group and the way others process as leaders in group-discussions.

The sharing of mentoring experiences in the group enables me to hear and comprehend how people grow in mentoring relationship according to their shared experiences. In one of my sessions a person shared if you truly want to see yourself as a leader, desire to have an out of body experience, whereby the leader steps back 15 feet from the experience and view the situation from a distance. I believe that at the roundtable I had the out of body experience. I saw myself as a Leader from a distance in an informational mode that led to the transformational process in the midst of dialogue on how to develop Leadership Character.

The Roundtable provided a medium for Leaders to express their learned knowledge and the groups a place of experiential expression. I believe that the roundtable initiated a platform for transformational Leadership.

Learning Exercise #16: A Guide to Defining Moments

This exercise is based on Badaracco's *Defining Moments.* Imagine that you are the Dean of the School of Business. You are facing this challenge. Answer these questions:

- What feelings and intuitions are coming into conflict in this situation?

- Which of the values that are in conflict are most deeply rooted in my life?

- What are the constraints that I must deal with?

- What is the most important value, and how can I infuse that value into the reality of this situation?

Learning Exercise #17: Moments of Discontinuity

In your small group, discuss how LeBron worked through his moment of discontinuity.

- What brought about this moment?

- What was the perceived gap between the real and ideal self?

- What was the internal struggle?

- What was the plan of action?

- What were the results?

Now, use the same set of questions and share a personal moment of discontinuity. It may be when you realized a new vision for your own leadership, when you embraced the reality of your own leadership patterns, or when you saw the gap between what you are and the leader you want to become.

- What brought about this moment in your life?

- What was your perception of your real and ideal self?

- What was your internal struggle?

- What was your plan of action?

- What were the results?

Learning Exercise #18: Living in the Tension

In your small group, answer these questions:

- **What is the ideal in Mary's heart?**

- **What is the messy reality of her job?**

- **What is the value that holds the tension between the two?**

- **What is Mary's creative strategy for implementing the value?**

- **What are the results for Mary and for those she leads?**

In your small group, let someone share their personal challenge of living in the tension. Help them articulate their heart's ideal, the messy reality, the needed value, and the creative strategy.

Learning Exercise #19: Lessons from the Long Road

In your small group, take a few moments to allow each person to draw a timeline of their leadership journey. Put triumphs and successes above the line, regrets and failures below the line. Some events and people may fit best on the line.

Let each person share whatever they would like from their own leadership journey. Let them share without interruption. When everyone has shared, discuss the following questions:

- **What do we have in common?**

- **What are the most important lessons we've learned?**

- **What kind of events had the greatest impact on shaping our character?**

Learning Exercise #20: We Need Each Other

In your small group, encourage each person to
share as they would like how your
"roundtable" of leaders has been a personal
benefit in their journey of leadership character
development

Chapter 7
Traveling Companions:
We Need Each Other

The fifth discovery in developing leadership character is "people." See Chapter 3 for a description of the five discoveries. You need people to help you at every step. Developing relationships that provide support make change possible. You need others to help you identify the leader you want to be and come to grips with the leader you are today.

Character development is a self-directed learning process. However, it cannot be done alone. Without others to give you encouragement and accountability, change will not happen.

One of the most common responses to the Leadership Roundtable was "We need this; we need a chance to talk together about leadership." Leaders can fall into a trap of isolation pressed on them through the demands and design of the role. A leader of character finds specific strategies to overcome the isolation and build strong networks with other leaders.

In this chapter, you will hear from three groups of leaders at different places on the journey. Students, middle managers, and seasoned leaders. Note the themes common to all three groups. Also, notice the themes unique to each group.

The following articles are reflections on "What I Learned from the Roundtable" by three students who have a great deal of leadership experience. These students served as facilitators for the nine leaders introduced in Chapter 5.

LEADERSHIP CHARACTER
Jonathon Dowdy
Master of Divinity Student
Ashland Theological Seminary

Our nation seems to be crying out for leaders to help guide us into the days ahead. Having seen some of our own religious and national leaders fall from grace we are faced with the reality that a leader is more than someone taking the lead and saying "follow me". Men and women that took the role of leader to obtain personal gain eventually lose the trust of the followers. Genuine character that is lived in the lives of our leaders is essential. As on of the speakers quoted, "We must be the change that we seek to produce." (Ghandi)

Leadership character starts with the individual. Self-examination allows a person to begin to incorporate characteristics that develop an effective leader. Traits such as courage, trust, integrity, credibility, confidence, compassion, honor and discipline. I am reminded that the Marines live by a code that is imbedded into the minds of each recruit and soldier; Duty, Honor, and Country. This mission is clear and their focus is set. The soldiers are trained to live by a set of standards that set them apart. They strive to serve honorably for the welfare of others.

Bill Perkins said that integrity in a leader speaks of someone who is whole or complete. They have taken the principles that govern their being and integrate them into every area of their life.

There can be good leaders that demonstrate character with a firm stand in their beliefs, but what is needed are leaders that have based their character on the Word of God and the principles that God has set for us as a standard.

If we are to train men and women into the leaders of tomorrow, we must begin by opening up the Word of God and presenting the standard that has been recorded for us to live by. God has given us many models that show us the unique ways in which his mission can be accomplished. Men and women do not have to be a particular type of person with a particular personality in order to be an effective leader. God uses "all" types of men and women with all types of personalities. An effective leader seeks to lead with truth, integrity, moral standards, honesty, and a true commitment.

When Christian beliefs and standards are lived personally, they flow into every area of our lives. Daily decisions influenced by our beliefs pour into our community that in turn overflow into our society with far reaching effects. The trust is that we will have men and women stepping up to take those leadership roles. It is imperative that the Christian community be bold and take their place as examples of moral character that is to be followed.

Relationships are one area that was stressed throughout the seminar. By building relationships we begin a foundation of trust. With trust as a base, a leader can form a team of people that will not only take ownership of the leaders vision but help them accomplish that vision.

I was very appreciative of being able to sit as a group and share experiences with one another. The idea of being able to hear what others have done in certain situations increases my learning and allows me to learn from others success and failures. It is my hope that I will be that courageous bold Christian that is willing to take a chance and step forward to lead in whatever capacity that the Lord directs. With Christ as my reason and the Word of God as my guide I have no reason to fear the challenge.

LEADERSHIP CHARACTER
Jaime Gillespie
Master of Leadership/Management Student
Master of Christian Education Student
Ashland Theological Seminary

Leadership is about more than simply setting vision, accomplishing goals, and leading people towards a destination which we can envision. More importantly than all of this, leadership is also about character. The character of a leader has a more profound impact on the

161

people and organizations with which they work, than any other thing they can do or produce. Character takes us to the heart of leadership: it is who we are as leaders, what we believe in, and what we will stand up for. It is also our internal compass to lead us to the eventual destination where we wish to end up.

When Ghandi said, "We must be the change we seek to produce", he hit at the heart of leadership character. A healthy, effective organization must begin with healthy, effective leaders. As a leader, I must be the change I seek to produce. If I want to develop an atmosphere of trust, *I* must trust the people I work with. If I want to encourage people to be courageous and creative, *I* must do so first! If I tell my organization that integrity is important, *I* need to be a leader of integrity.

I learned that leadership character is essentially influenced by and impacted by relationships. Leaders must have healthy, open, and honest relationships with those around them. These relationships will build a foundation for the trust that is absolutely essential to leadership. Leaders must be willing to open up their lives to those around them, and to build relationships that transcend the office place, organization, or work week. Followers need to know that we truly care about them: as employees, contributors to our common goals, and friends.

One thing that impacted me during this Roundtable was when Paul Blease said, "When who you are fuses with what you do, the power it creates is immeasurable." This reminds me of the Biblical teachings about Spiritual Gifts. If who we are (our gifts, talents, personalities, experiences, passions, and abilities) fuses with what we do (our work, our ministry, our hobbies, etc.), an amazing amount of power can be created! What a change this could mean for our organizations! As leaders, we need identify and acknowledge who we are. We need to be aware of our weaknesses and limitations, and surround ourselves with people who can fill in those gaps. By trying to be who we are not, we not only risk our own identity and health, but also the effectiveness and health of our organization.

The most powerful lesson I learned about leadership character was on perspective. A leader needs to have a clear vision and goals, but these need to be based on a perspective of life that is larger than "here and now." Leaders need to look beyond what will be effective today, what will be gratifying and lucrative right now, and what will makes us happy at this stage of our lives. A leader needs to look beyond the present, to a point in the future when work will be behind us, children will be grown and on their own, and life is fading away. From this perspective, a leader must ask, "What will make me look back on my life and be satisfied and content? What will I value at that time?"

When we can look at our lives and our jobs from this greater perspective, we can learn to evaluate what we do and who we are in a much different light. We can begin building the foundations of our lives on solid ground, and we can "set our ladder against the correct wall." If we can do this now, when life is over and we have climbed to the top of the ladder, we will not be disappointed. Instead of "climbing the ladder of success only to find that it is leaning against the wrong wall" (Paul Blease), we will look back on our life and say, "What a trip!" We can then go to meet God with no regrets, no disappointments, and with the knowledge that we remained true to our leadership character, that we didn't compromise our identity or our integrity, and we stayed the course which Christ had called us to. Then, and only then, will we know true contentment and peace.

LEADERSHIP CHARACTER
Bob Grover
Church Planter
Seminary Student
Ashland Theological Seminary

A month has past and I sit and reflect realizing that some things have already faded away awhile others still stand clear. The stuff that you remember a month later tends to be the "keepers". I am left with some one-liners that will sit with me for some time to come.

Position, prominence, and public notoriety are no substitution for character.

Trust is won slowly, lost quickly, and not easily rebuilt, if at all.

Integrity, relationship, and competence combine to form trust.

Trust, combined with vision and passion, creates leadership.

Mission gets us "on the boat" with a purpose; a reason, a cause.

Vision gives us "a destination": a goal to accomplish that gives the mission direction and fulfillment

163

Leaders have to do more than manage the status quo: they have to guide everyone into change with a purpose

Principles are spiritual truths that are universal and impervious to what you think!

Truly diversified groups create the opportunity to see more sides of the challenges we face and this more often leads to better solutions.

Every great journey takes place outside the comfort zone. If you are not outside the comfort zone, you probably aren't growing. Your comfort zone is either expanding or contracting but it is never static.

The last statement is the one I would like to focus on. When I agreed to be a small group facilitator my perception was that I would be rubbing shoulders with a few other pastors. I thought it would be a good opportunity for me to stretch my horizons. and admittedly, get a free lunch out of the deal.

I was surprised to find myself in the middle of a gathering of greatness. The rooms reeked of leadership yet, not a single person that I met came across as arrogant or vain. I was in amongst leaders from all walks of life who were eager to learn despite the fact they were already accomplished in their fields. They were there to stretch their comfort zones! They were curious about what they might need to learn; ready to be transparent for the sake of improvement and willing to share their triumphs and failures.

Were these people hand picked to attend because they possessed unique leadership character already? It would seem that everyone there came not knowing what they were going to learn but at the very least knowing that they were going to be challenged to learn something new. They were all ready and willing to be stretched.

As I look at the word "leadership" from a perspective of stretching our comfort zones and expanding our horizons, I realize the root word is "to lead," to go ahead of! Leadership implicitly demands forward movement! I learned from our shared experiences that a good guidance system for forward moving leadership is frequent evaluation: to constantly challenged the way we look at our own world. We always need to look from new perspectives.

164

- Are we headed in the right direction?
- Do we have a worthy destination? (vision)
- Are we analyzing the failures along the journey?
- Is there a better way? A simpler way?
- Are we truly serving those we lead along the way?
- Are we good stewards of the human resources who are entrusted to us?
- Are we being accountable to those we lead?
- Are we being honest with our followers, our God, and ourselves?

If we are not regularly asking questions like this, we fall into an oxymoron called "stagnant leadership." This is nothing more that management of the status quo in disguise!

Consider this: When we first step out in faith to follow Christ, it is the ultimate experience of stretching our comfort zone. We initially take steps uniquely placed on the foundations of truth and faith for the single purpose of learning to follow. But, sooner or later, by default, we become leaders in some capacity. That's because leadership is integrated into the life of a maturing Christian As we mature in the faith, we all become leaders because we eventually convert from the disciple to the teacher.

I learned that when we lead, we have a responsibility to those who follow us. Whether it be in the arena of the business world, the church, or in government: we must lead with the perspective that we are called by God and we are only empowered to lead by His Holy Spirit and Divine intervention. As we process this, we can then begin to grasp the awesome responsibilities we have to develop, maintain, and grow our leadership character.

It comes to mind that every time Moses encountered God, he was challenged to lead his people (spiritually or physically) as well as commissioned with a task that only God could accomplish through him. God does the same to leaders even still today. We can expect that God will always be stretching our comfort zones by challenging us to follow His son Jesus Christ in faith, doing things that bring Him honor and glory in whatever we do in life. That includes every aspect of our life.

I have learned by participation in this conference that leadership is a life long learning process down a road best traveled with trusting companions. When we come together for conferences like this, the Holy

Spirit works in the community of believers to encourage leadership character in each one of us. We are met with intentional challenges that better equip us for the unforeseen challenges that lay ahead in daily living. The inexperienced bring fresh perspectives and the experienced bring sage advice. The diversity of parallel experiences also brings to the table unique perspectives from which to view things.

By risking and being a little transparent in this type if setting, we gain much. In submitting ourselves to one another we share, learn, build relationships, and we energize and encourage one another.

What a great God we serve who would bring us all together in an environment that gives us the tools to develop leadership character.

Middle Management

A group of administrators from Ashland Theological Seminary facilitated the small group discussion at the Roundtable. They worked with the presenters (Introduced in Chapter 1) and practitioners (Introduced in Chapters 2 and 3). These administrators hold positions of middle management and exhibit strong leadership skills in directing their personal areas of responsibility as well as influencing the direction of the seminary.

LEADERSHIP CHARACTER
Shawn Oliver, Director
Curriculum and Academic Support Services,
Master of Divinity Program
Ashland Theological Seminary

The Round-Table Convocation on "Leadership Character" held at The Sandberg Leadership Center on October 25-27, 2001, was both encouraging and challenging for me. Those in attendance brought with them their various backgrounds, their success stories, their struggles,

166

their frustrations, and their hopes for learning about and living out leadership character. I find it encouraging that people in a variety of professions and with varying backgrounds can find some common agreement on the characteristics of leadership character. I appreciated the spirit of the convocation and the willingness of all to rise up and say that character is essential for an effective leader.

The major theme presenters each shared on an area of passion and expertise. They challenged my thinking and my actions. The group discussion sessions gave us an excellent opportunity to wrestle with the topic of leadership character. For me, leadership character includes what I believe, how I act, and how my beliefs and actions affect my relationships with others as I function in a leadership role.

As a leader I believe in trustworthiness, integrity, authenticity, and other essential leadership character qualities that can only be developed out of my relationship with Jesus Christ. In order to have people who follow, I as a leader must have the trust of the people, which is built over time. A leader must be both believable and trustworthy. Living a life of character is essential to a fulfilled life. God designed us with an ability to lead a life of character because of our connection with him. Sin entered the picture, which now leaves right and wrong, treatment of others, leading with integrity, etc.? I must continually evaluate how I am responding in these areas. Leadership character must be at the very core of who I am. Apart from my relationship with Jesus Christ and his leadership model, I have no frame of reference on which to build leadership character.

LEADERSHIP CHARACTER
Vickie Taylor
Director, Technical Resources
Ashland Theological Seminary

When I first thought about this room full of leaders from all across the country, I wondered why I was even in the same room. It suddenly occurred to me that leadership is not about position and power; it was about character. I, too, had something to contribute to the study of leadership for I am a leader in my own right, not a leader of position and power but a person that leads by character. This is exactly what we are studying and writing about, leadership character. What makes one person a leader and not another? Or, is the question we should be asking,

"Is everyone a leader?" What are the leadership characteristics that label a person a leader? Are we looking for leaders or are we looking for leaders with character? From the group discussions that occurred over this weekend, answers to these questions began to develop for me and for others who may be pondering what the title "Leadership Character" really means.

From the first night we gathered together in the Sandberg Leadership Center, I sensed a different air in the room; it was an air of anticipation and excitement. We were on a new adventure, surrounded by people who were all Christians yet held different positions in life. Some gathered were business leaders who trained others to be great leaders, some were owner of businesses, some were politicians and others were deans of seminaries and business schools. Though all had different positions in life, all were passionate about what they do in their lives.

Some leaders lead by shear power of the position they possess, but others are leaders who are leaders because they posses the qualities of a genuine leader. This was the type of leader who attended this conference. These genuine leaders are people who have developed strategies and skills that are necessary for successful leadership and they were about to share their insight with all who were gathered. We were learning together in community.

The skills and strategies we need to develop and grow into better leaders can be found in the pages of Scripture and particularly in the life of Jesus. When we look at a list that includes such qualities as commitment, integrity, faith, trust, credibility, competence, and discipline, we see Jesus. Submission to God to develop the characteristics of Jesus is what we, as Christians, are called to in our faith journey.

When I was growing up, I was the oldest of three girls. As the oldest, I believed my leadership rose was clear; it was my job to take the risks, discover that worked and what didn't, and then teach the right way to my younger sisters. To me, this was what leadership was about. This weekend clarified for me one crucial error in my thinking. Where do they learn to take risks? How do they develop their own leadership character?

In our country alone, we have a 200 plus year history of leadership. Even today, as the lessons are learned and passed down, we are not any further along in leadership development than we were 200 years ago. Why is that?

In my opinion, much has to do with leadership character. We have tried to define character in secular terms. What does trustworthy really mean outside of Jesus' example? Where is the line of integrity drawn when we manipulate the line to meet our own needs and desires? Is humility understood outside of understanding Jesus' role in our lives?

When I look at the list of essentials of leadership character, it appears tht this is a list of character traits that must be developed over time with patience and persistence. We are not born into great leadership; we are developed into leaders. Whether we become good leaders or great leaders depends on how much time and energy we devote to the air of leadership. In many of our sessions the key concepts of discipline, commitment, evaluation, and practice were reoccurring. We used words such as mentor and coach that are words that signify training and teaching. All this is framed around the guidance of the Scriptures and the model of Jesus Christ. It appears to be easy! Obviously it is not.

Great leadership is difficult because we are human. We want to follow our own agendas, we want to allow our egos to be the guide, and we want to bend integrity to meet our specific needs. Character development in leadership goes hand and hand with discipleship. As we transform into the image of Christ, we learn about character. From this perfect model, we can grown into leaders of integrity, leaders that keep the vision flaming, and leaders that are key examples to others.

If we can take our "failures" in leadership and transform them into lessons learned, we have just developed and grown in character. Instead of judging successes and failures just on society's definitions and begin to transform risk-taking into grown lessons we can pass on this valuable information to others. The commitment and discipline of learning is a constant necessity for leadership character development. Our goal is to be on a constant journey, first to Christlikeness and then to take our lessons from Christ and instill them into our own understanding of leadership character. Only through this exact process can we become leaders who can produce change, good change, in our society. We must ask ourselves these two basic questions and then reflect upon them until we can honestly answer them:

Are we exercising the leadership we are capable of to produce good change in our society?

169

Are we preparing leaders for the future that will produce change in our society?

If we can wrestle honestly with these questions, we are on the journey to leadership development. What is our leadership all about if not to bring about change that was called forth in our lives through Jesus Christ?

LEADERSHIP CHARACTER
Bob Rosa
Director of Admissions
Ashland Theological Seminary

Learning is a life long process through a range of means and methods, and this seminar was a microcosm of the process, with a variety of facilitating events. I learned from each keynote speaker, I learned as I listened to each small group presenter, and I learned while I was facilitating small group discussion: three different, but all effective, methods of learning.

I learned that leadership character is a process that is ongoing. To be a leader requires a particular character and personality. Some individuals are more naturally born and gifted with leadership character, but at the same time character can be changed, learned and developed. The only difference is that it comes easier for some and it requires more concerted effort for others.

But what comes first, the chicken or the egg? Or, in this case, the leader or the character? Can I be in a leadership position first, and then begin to work on my character? Or, does my character allow me to function in such a way that I move into a position of leadership? The more I reflect on this dichotomy, I must conclude that there is a two-pronged conclusion. Ideally, my character will motivate my actions. In turn, my actions or behaviors will produce results, which will culminate with me being seen as a leader, and ultimately placed into a leadership position. This is the ideal. However, the reality is that a number of people in positions of leadership are not in that place because of character, but because of results. Furthermore, their successful results may be the result of a lack of character.

I learned that my desire to be a leader with character could result in come conflict. I will be in the minority, and the majority, since they

170

lack character, may respond to me with some unwelcome methods. In fact, some people will be downright rude.

This seminar reminded me that my leadership character formation begins with my personal spiritual formation. Repeatedly throughout the seminar mention was made regarding spiritual formation. A personal ongoing relationship with Jesus Christ is the foundation to developing leadership character. Spending time in prayer, Bible reading and moments of meditation are essential for leadership character formation. Simply stated, being formed into the image of Christ results in modeling Jesus' attributes, which includes leadership. Furthermore, out of this relationship with Jesus comes a vision statement.

The vision comes from him, not something conjured up by a person working out of his or her own being. In fact, the vision is given to the leader by Jesus to be implemented by the leader and the people empowered by him/her. Moreover, as the leader maintains this intimate relationship with Christ, another quality emerges which, in turn, develops character. That quality is perseverance. I learned that a person can not be a successful leader unless he or she develops perseverance as a character trait. It will be this gift of perseverance that will enable the leader to see the vision through.

Here is a simple definition I learned that describes a leader: a leader is someone who can influence people. He or she motivates others to grab hold of his or her vision and make it their own. How are people influenced to catch the leaders' vision? Here lies another quality of leadership character. The leader must be a person of honesty and authenticity. And as a result of these qualities, the leader is trusted. Furthermore, the leader maintains trust based on three important issues. First, the leader must be a person of relationships; they must feel comfortable and natural being around people and interacting with them. Second, the leader must be a person of integrity. Third, the leader with character must exude competence. People must be able to observe the leader be successful in leading. The leader needs to be able to model goals and plans.

Paul Blease made some significant statements as he talked about leadership character. He said, "When who you are fuses with what you do, the result is unlimited power and influence." Confidence grows out of the knowledge of who I am in Christ, and purpose grows out of the vision Christ shares with the leader through an intimate relationship.

The most important principle I learned is that trying to be a leader with character is challenging. This reminds me of the first sentence from Scott Peck's book, *A Road Less Traveled*, "Life is difficult." Walking the narrow road of leadership character, otherwise known as servant leadership, is difficult. However, this seminar also reinforced for me that although difficult, leadership character development is not impossible. I'm encouraged by the words of the apostle Paul in Ephesians 3:20, "I can do all things through Christ who strengthens me." Leadership character is formed and facilitated as the leader functions out of an intimate relationship with Christ.

For Reflection...
> *"Godly character demands careful action, authenticity and integrity... both personally and in relationship with those with whom I am in community."*—Phil Kizzee

Seasoned Leaders

Our Roundtable presenters (Introduced in Chapter 2) prepared reflections of their personal learning through the roundtable experience. They were specifically asked to address the crisis of leadership character.

For Reflection...
> *"Balancing character and competency must be a daily priority if integrity is to be achieved and maintained."*
> --Dr. Charles Lake

"THE CRISIS OF LEADERSHIP CHARACTER"
Lovett H. Weems, Jr.
President of Saint Paul School of Theology
in Kansas City, Missouri

Participating in the *"Addressing the Crisis of Leadership Character"* conference at Sandberg Leadership Center served to confirm some important understandings about the components of leadership and leadership character, as well as to remind me of other dimensions that are easily forgotten.

Everything we do begins with mission and vision. Using a boat and trip example, one speaker spoke of the mission as "why we are in the boat" and the vision as "where we are going." These "why" and "where" questions face us throughout a lifetime. We must know the purpose of our lives and the purpose of our organizations, yet that is not enough by itself. We must also know the appropriate next step or destination for us, given the purpose. Mission by itself never moves to meaningful action. Vision also can become a mere nice idea if separated from the mission that gives it meaning in the first place.

Communicating the mission and vision in simple and compelling imagery is also crucial. A physicist who received a Nobel Prize was quoted as saying, "If it is not simple, it is not true." Great leaders of character found ways to capture their visions in simple, though powerful, ways. The illustrations given at the conference included:

Martin Luther King, Jr. – "equal opportunity"
Abraham Lincoln – "preserve the union"
Mahatma Gandhi – "independence"
Jesus – "love"

Simple does not equate with easy, we were reminded, though there is great power in a significant concept captured very clearly and succinctly.

Leaders of character do not act alone. The myth of the lone leader acting as a brave individual does not match the story of great leaders. In fact, leaders are only leaders in relationship to a larger community. Leaders gather around them teams that together are much stronger and wiser than any individual leader. One speaker told of a frequently-used exercise that makes this point. Participants are each asked to make a list of all the vegetables they can name. Then the participants are divided into groups, and each group compiles a list of

173

vegetables. Invariably, the best score by an individual is surpassed by the number of vegetables named by the group with the *worst* score!

Although the combination of competency and character was a major aspect of the presentation I made at the conference, the importance of these two dimensions of leadership in combination with each other was taken to new heights by the contributions of others. The statement made in a conference presentation that will stay with me for a long time is: "Some leaders have competency skills that take them beyond where their character will permit them to remain."

The distinction made by Bill Perkins between a principle and a value helps me understand why it is so easy to accept a principle and yet not find it embodied in one's life. He said that a principle is something that is always true. It becomes a value for us when we have internalized the principle. For example, "exercise will lead to a healthier life" is a principle. It becomes a value for us only when we build this principle into our lives through regular exercise.

Another concept presented that was intriguing to me was the idea that "we all stop growing at some point in our childhood and put an adult covering on our lives."

Richard Parrott's words of inspiration throughout the conference were some of the most inspiring contributions to our deliberations. Using scripture, he had just the word that leaders of character need to keep going. The theme that seemed to run through his remarks was the importance of taking that faithful next step. From Isaiah 40:31, Richard reminded us that mounting up and soaring like eagles is an exhilarating experience but one that occurs seldom in our lives. Running in such a way as to achieve great victories that result in marvelous celebrations are thrilling, but they certainly do not occur every day or even frequently. And yet, the daily perseverance of walking, taking one step after the other, comes last in the scriptural ordering and is perhaps the greatest achievement for leaders.

One of the most rewarding benefits of the conference was seeing the passion and energy for the subject of leadership character exhibited by so many different people from different life situations. Clearly, this is a subject of great importance and timeliness for many people today.

"THE CRISIS OF LEADERSHIP CHARACTER"

Valerie K. Brown, CPA
Executive Director and founder of the
Church Financial Management and Leadership Institute, Assistant
Professor of Management at the
Samuel D. Proctor School of Theology

The Round Table Convocation on *Leadership Character* was truly God-inspired and God-centered. All the speakers, participants, and facilitators were focused and ready to hear from God on the issues of leadership character in not only their individual lives but in the lives of leaders everywhere.

What stood out most profoundly to me as I listened to not only the speakers, but the participants during the break-out sessions, is that everyone agreed on a similar list of traits and qualities that one would expect leaders to possess. Some of the traits mentioned over and over were:

Trust – the foundation of effective leaders; easily and quickly lost, but won slowly

Competency – ability to lead

Character – what you do and say when no one is looking; the "real" you

Vision – the ability to see what others can not see; yet, the ability to inspire others to follow anyway

Accountability – accepting the responsibility for all decisions and actions

God-centered and God-focused – remembering to keep God first in all matters

What also stood out for me was that while everyone could agree on the list of traits and qualities, we all recognized that leaders are human like the rest of us and subject to failures. The difference between a leader and a follower, is that the leader keeps on trying even after failing several times. A major point, however, was made relevant to keeping leaders on track and helping to reduce the number of character flaws that could potentially bring demise to ministries. That point was the creation of an "accountability group." The accountability group would meet once a month simply to pose six questions to each of its members. Given the nature of each question, it is evident that members of the accountability group must be made up of members who respect and trust each other greatly. The purpose of the accountability group is to give leaders someone to be accountable to for their actions.

The six questions posed deal with the areas of morality, faithfulness to spouse, faithfulness to God, and faithfulness to financial matters. The sixth question, however, is much more sole-defining. The sixth and final question asked each time is, "Have you just lied to me with your answers to the first five questions?" That to me, was a powerful question and outstanding way to offer self-conviction to leaders.

It is evident in our society today, that being a leader, especially in a faith-based entity is very difficult. As discussed in several of the sessions, people hold religious leaders to a higher level of moral behavior than their secular counterparts. The limelight, therefore, shines brighter and the scrutiny is much closer. The accountability group was a wonderful response to this dilemma for leaders.

Finally, as we talk about leadership character and development, it was quite evident that the need for Leadership Centers that focus on developing leaders of great character is definitely needed. Seminaries and Schools of theology are still debating on their role in the delivery of classes in leadership. Leadership Centers will be able to address the needs of leaders in a way that seminaries and schools of theology will not be able to do.

We have entered into the twenty-first century and there is a great need for great leaders. Leaders who can incorporate all the traits and skills we articulated yet are grounded with a strong character. In the words of Bill Perkins, we don't need leaders "whose competencies have taken them to places where their character can not sustain them."

"THE CRISIS OF LEADERSHIP CHARACTER"
Bill Perkins
Founder and president of the Million Mighty Men, author of *Awaken the Leader Within* and contributor to the *Leadership Bible*

Dwight D. Eisenhower defined leadership as, "the art of getting someone else to do something you want done because he wants to do it." If you accept that definition of leadership (it's my favorite) then you're buying into two truths. First, you're a leader. When I make that observation at business seminars I'm immediately greeted with looks of disbelief. Undaunted, I ask the audience a very simple question. "Have you ever been in a situation at work or home where you tried to get someone else to do something?" Immediately everyone raises their hand and nods their head.

According to Eisenhower's definition, you become a leader the moment you attempt to get someone else to do something. Since that's the case the issue isn't, are you a leader? You are! The issue is how can you lead more effectively.

Answering that question brings us to the second truth issuing out of Eisenhower's definition, namely, leaders are made not born. Since leadership is an art, effective leadership is the result of hard work not genes. So whether you've recently been thrust into a leadership role and feel as out of place as a turtle at a road race, or you're heading up a Fortune 500 Company, you need to sharpen your leadership skills.

Learning to lead is like mastering a musical instrument—there are fundamental chords that can be studied, practiced and mastered. I've discovered whether I'm meeting with the CEO of a billion dollar company or counseling a mother or father—the fundamentals of leadership are the same and must be mastered. While natural talent is a shortcut to musical excellence, it doesn't replace hard work. Similarly, while some men and women have a natural capacity for leadership, they too must study the art and work hard at mastering the fundamentals. Those with less innate talent can still excel as leaders if they're willing to study the basics and put them into practice. Becoming an effective leader demands rigorous study and hard work.

The Leadership Model of Jesus

In three-and-a-half years Jesus established a movement that has lasted twenty centuries and involved over a billion people. He did this without traveling far from home, writing a book, leading an army, or holding a political office.

How did one man so significantly impact the world? He did it by personally training and utilizing techniques we can study, practice and eventually master. His strategy wasn't the result of a lucky toss of the dice but of a well thought out plan by a man with sterling character and finely honed leadership skills. He didn't succeed because he recruited a team of superstars, but because he passed on to his team the character traits and skills they would need to pass on to others.

Jesus didn't buy into the separation of character and competence in a leader. In fact, his harshest words were aimed at leaders who looked

177

competent on the outside but smelled rotten on the inside.[6] With that truth in mind, how can followers of Jesus affectively address the crisis of leadership character today?

Competency Builds on Character

Based on the interaction at the round table I'd like to make several suggestions.

First, we must develop an ongoing awareness that it is our relationship with Jesus Christ that is the source of sterling character. On the night before his death Jesus told his disciples, "I am the vine and you are the branches. If a man remains in me and I in him, he will bear much fruit; apart from me you can do nothing" (John 15:5). We must strive to live in an ongoing conscious awareness of the life of Christ that dwells in us. And we must daily seek him through Bible reading and prayer. One message that repeatedly came through from every round-table discussion: The cultivation of a growing personal relationship with Christ is the foundation upon which a leader's character must be built.

Second, as leaders we must consistently seek to be the same on the inside as we appear to be on the outside. That is, we must be men and women of integrity. How can we become such people? It begins with the recognition that as members of a fallen race our hearts are prone to seek out evil. Furthermore, when we commit evil deeds our natural tendency is to cover our tracks—like robbers fleeing the scene of a crime. What we must realize is that we're running through snow and ultimately others will see our tracks—and even if they don't—God does.

Since that's the case, we must be brutally honest with a few close friends and ourselves. Such transparency provides a harness for our most dangerous appetites and prevents us from acting out in ways that undermine our leadership skills.

Leaders of integrity are also teachable. They are open to criticism and willing to change. They know that followers aren't looking for perfect leaders. But they do want leaders they feel are in touch with who they are and are in the process of growing themselves.

Linked to integrity is the third element we must cultivate: accountability. Leaders of character realize they need to be accountable,

---

[6] Bill Perkins, *Awaken the Leader Within,* Zondervan Publishing House, Grand Rapids, 2000, pp. 13-14.

not just for their personal behavior, but for the resources under their charge. By putting into place checks and balances an entire organization is protected from the accidental oversights of team members as well as those seeking dishonest gain. Of course, such accountability indicates a willingness on the part of a leader to relinquish control and freedom.

Fourth, leaders of character must seek out settings where they can interact with other leaders. While it's true that eagles don't fly in flocks, leaders must occasionally do just that. One of the great lessons I learned from the leadership roundtable was that other leaders possess priceless insight. The perspective, problem solving techniques, and systems they utilize are invaluable. Their devotion to the development of character and competency are both instructional and motivational.

Finally, we must remember that ultimately it is our character that provides the foundation for our leadership skills. And while a leader's skills may take him beyond what his character will sustain— eventually unless he cultivates godly character—those who follow will be gravely disappointed. The safest insurance against building a team or organization that sinks is building it on the foundation of godly character.

For Reflection...
   "No leader is perfect."—Shawn Oliver

Biographies

PAUL BLEASE

Paul Blease, Director of Advanced Training at Solomon, Smith Barney in New York. Paul has been working in the industry for 20 years and is in charge of training all of the top producers (stock brokers and managers) for the company. Paul received his B.A. in Political Science and Philosophy from the University of Arizona.

He married his college sweetheart and has been married for 19 years. Paul and his wife have 3 children, Shannon 16, T.J. 11 and David 7. They have lived in seven states during the last 15 years and currently live in North Cauldwell, N. J.

VALERIE K. BROWN

Dr. Valerie K. Brown, CPA is Executive Director and founder of the Church Financial Management and Leadership Institute located in Chesapeake, VA. Dr. Brown did her undergraduate and graduate work at Virginia State University, Petersburg, VA and the College of William & Mary, Williamsburg, VA. She received her doctorate degree in Business Management from the Weatherhead School of Management, Case Western Reserve University, Cleveland, Ohio.

Dr. Brown also serves as Assistant Professor of Management at the Samuel D. Proctor School of Theology, Virginia Union University, Richmond, VA where she teaches Church Administration and Finance at the graduate level. She also teaches Leadership in the Doctor of Ministry Program.

ROD BUSHEY

Rod Bushey has been teaching choral music at Howell High School in Howell, Michigan for the past thirty years. His choir is the largest single program in the high school with over four hundred forty students enrolled in eight performing ensembles. His students have developed a reputation for outstanding choral performances at concerts, consistently high marks at choral competitions, and numerous appearances both locally and throughout the state of Michigan. His 100-voice a cappella Choir has toured for the past twenty seven years in the states of Wisconsin, Ohio, Michigan, Indiana, Illinois, Pennsylvania, New Jersey, New York and Canada. The Howell Choirs have produced six full-length recordings across the past 30 years.

In 1999, Howell Public Schools named Mr. Bushey, "Teacher of the Year." Rod earned a B.A. in Music Education from Olivet Nazarene University in 1972 where he is president of the Olivet Alumni Association. He also holds a Masters in Music Education from Michigan State University [1980]. Beyond the public school, Rod held a Minister of Music position for twenty-five years in four different Nazarene churches, with 19 years of service at Detroit First Church of the Nazarene. He is married to Cindy, also a graduate of Olivet Nazarene University. Their children are Tricia [28} and Greg [26], both Olivet grads and married living in Dayton, Ohio and Royal Oak, Michigan, respectively.

JAYNE L. COOPER

Jayne L. Cooper serves as President of the Ashland Area Chamber of Commerce in Ashland, Ohio. An Ashland County native, Jayne returned to the community in 1992 to assume her current position. Prior to that, she served as Vice President with the Wooster Area Chamber of Commerce for five years. She served previously as Assistant Controller of a major regional oil and gas company, and began her career as a Student Services Administrator at South Dakota State University.

Jayne says that Chamber work is the perfect combination of what she loved in all of her previous positions. As a self-described private enterprise nut, Cooper enjoys working with and serving a variety of people with a myriad of needs, but always with the goal of helping people flourish in the world of work. "People buy from people, people invest in people, people help people," she says. Investment and return on investment have the same common denominator, people! As a chamber leader, she gets to serve human needs.

Cooper is a graduate of Capital University and Institutes for Organization Management at the University of Georgia. She achieved the designation of Accredited Professional from Chamber of Commerce Executives of Ohio in 1997, and in 2001 was name the Professional of the Year.

She serves on various Boards at a state and local level, and counts her volunteer service as important for personal more than professional reasons. She is a musician and a YMCA junkie.

JONATHAN DOWDY

A student at Ashland Theological Seminary, Jonathan will be graduating with the class of 2002 with his Master's of Divinity degree. Upon graduation he will enter the ministry as a pastor in the Brethren Church where he will serve with his wife Kathleen and their sons Luke, Tyler, and Samuel.

Jonathan served seven years in the US Air Force as a Titan II Missile Specialist and Avionics Specialist on the F-16 Fighting Falcon. After leaving the military he spent ten years with the Space Program at NASA Kennedy Space Center. His career included service with the Shuttle Launch and Recovery Teams for 72 flight missions for both the military and civilian sector.

Experienced in Christian Camping programming, for the past ten years, Jonathan has served as teacher, director and manager of a summer youth camping program. While a student at ATS, Jonathan and his wife served two years as the coordinators for Ashland's BalloonFest, an annual community event featuring hot air balloon races and festival activities. He has worked at the YMCA as an aquatics instructor and lifeguard. He serves as pastor of the Savannah Presbyterian Church in Savannah, OH.

E. LeBRON FAIRBANKS

Dr. E. LeBron Fairbanks, President of Mount Vernon Nazarene University, earned his undergraduate degree at Trevecca Nazarene University in 1964. He received three master's degrees -- the M.A. from Scarritt University in 1967, the M.Div. from the Nazarene Theological Seminary in 1970, and the M.Th. from Princeton Theological Seminary in 1971.

In 1976, he was designated a Fellow in Pastoral Leadership Education by Princeton Theological Seminary, and earned the D.Min. degree from Nazarene Theological Seminary in 1978. Dr. Fairbanks is a

1991 graduate of the Harvard University Institute of Educational Management.

Recently, Dr. Fairbanks was on sabbatical as a Research Fellow at the Yale University Divinity School. Dr. Fairbanks was involved in local church ministries in Tennessee and Pennsylvania for fourteen years, after which he became Academic Dean in 1978 for the European Nazarene College near Schaffhausen, Switzerland. In 1982, he became Associate Professor of Christian Education and Lay Ministry Development, and Coordinator of the Master of Ministry program at Southern Nazarene University.

Two years later, Dr. Fairbanks was elected President of the Asia Pacific Nazarene Theological Seminary in Manila, Philippines, where he served until accepting the presidency of Mount Vernon Nazarene University in July 1989. Under his leadership, APNTS received full accreditation from the Asian Theological Association and was granted "recognition" status (accreditation) by the Philippine government Department of Education. APNTS was the first graduate theological seminary not associated with a university in the Philippines to receive this recognition.

Dr. Fairbanks has written two books for a Bible study series and numerous articles for Nazarene publications. He has traveled to 33 countries worldwide and serves on a variety of community, state, national, and international boards. His article on "Institutional Collaboration as Institutional Strategy" has appeared in several publications. From 1995-1998, Dr. Fairbanks served as chair of a Church of the Nazarene Council of Education subcommittee developing a strategic plan for networking and collaboration. He was one of two North Americans recently appointed to serve on an international ministerial training standards committee for the Church of the Nazarene International. He is a member of the writing team for the Nazarene Education Manifesto, and the Team CIS (Confederation of Independent States) teaching and writing project.

Dr. Fairbanks was a presenter at the Johannesburg 2000, in Johannesburg, South Africa, an international conference of Nazarene educators worldwide. He serves on the executive committee of the Ohio Foundation of Independent Universities. He is a presidential mentor in the Executive Leadership Institute, Council for Christian Colleges and Universities.

185

Dr. Fairbanks was born in Chattanooga, Tennessee. He married Anne in 1962 and they have one son, Stephen.

MARK A. FARMER

Marc A. Farmer is bi-vocational. His leadership and management experience is derived from serving more than 23 years in the United States Marshals Service, US Department of Justice. Currently he is serving in Washington, D.C. holding the position of Chief Inspector of Judicial Protective Services, managing a nearly 180 million-program, representing a nationwide protective force of more than 4,000 officers. He has served a speaker, instructor and course developer for Federal, State, and Local Police Agencies, to include: DEA, FBI, IRS, ATF, the Organized Crime Drug Task Force, the Attorney Generals Advocacy Institute, the Federal Judiciary, and Congregations and various Church Organizations throughout the United States.

His experience in leadership and management includes more than 22 years in Ministry; to include serving on the Ministerial Staff of various churches, Associate Pastor at Euclid Ave. Church of God in Cleveland Ohio and Long Reach Church of God in Columbia, Maryland. Currently serving as the Founder and Senior Pastor of Oakland Mills Church of God in Columbia, Maryland. Outstanding awards include the Commissioner's Citation from the Baltimore City Police Department, and a number of performance awards. He is also an award recipient of two Communicator Awards for video production.

Accomplishments in education include receiving a Master's Degree from Ashland Theological Seminary, Ashland, Ohio, Master's of Science in National Resource Strategy from The National Defense University, commonly known as the "War College"' Washington, D.C., and a Doctor of Ministry Degree in Urban Ministry from Wesley Theological Seminary; Washington, D.C.

FREDERICK J. FINKS

Dr. Finks has served as president of Ashland Theological Seminary from 1982. He has also served pastorates in Ohio and Indiana and has served on various boards, district and national for the Brethren Church. His experience also includes serving on the National Association

186

of Evangelicals Board of Administrators, 1984-2000. Dr. Finks is a consultant for church growth and planning and has conducted over 100 seminars on leadership and administration the United States, South America and Asia. Dr. Finks is also a Board member of the South America Theological Seminary, Argentina.

Dr. Finks received a B.A. in Psychology, 1969 from Ashland University and a Master of Divinity from Ashland Theological Seminary, 1972. His Doctor of Ministry degree is from Fuller Theological Seminary, 1980. Post Doctoral studies were done in Cambridge, England.

Community service includes Rotary International, 1986-1996 and a member of the Ashland Area Chamber of Commerce and Board member, 1998-2002. Dr. Finks served as Chair of the Chamber Board in 2001. Fred and his wife, Holly have been married for 33 years and they have two children and two grandchildren.

JAIMIE GILLESPIE

I am 25 years old, and have been a Christian since I was 9 years old. For as long as I can remember, I wanted to be doctor. But God had other plans. God called me to full-time ministry when I was 19 years old; but, like Jonah, I didn't want to go. After struggling through a pre-medicine/biology undergraduate degree at Ashland University, I finally gave in to God and enrolled at Ashland Theological Seminary. In December 2001, I will complete my Masters in Leadership/Management, and Christian Education.

I currently serve as the National Youth Leader for The Brethren Church, and as Content Manager for TeamCE.com, and on-line youth ministry resource through Christian Endeavor International. God has blessed me and my life has been immeasurably enriched by these incredible opportunities. I have had the chance to train youth leaders all over the country, as well as to lead young people, to help them discover their own leadership potential, and to walk beside them as they make a difference in our world. I can only say that God has made my every dream come true. I may not be a doctor; by I am still helping people every day, maybe even in a more profound way.

I am engaged to a wonderful man and will be married in September of 2002. My fiancé, Bryan Parsons is a high school science teacher, a swim coach, and an all-around incredible man. We plan to stay in Ashland, Ohio and start a family.

ARDEN GILMER

A native Hoosier, I was born in Huntington, Indiana in 1943. Other than my salvation, parents who loved the Lord, loved each other, and loved their children were God's greatest gift to me. Though I did not recognize it during my childhood, I now know that they laid a strong foundation for me. The Lord called my father off of his farm and into the full time ministry when I was ten years old. Some preacher's kids have a strong need to rebel. I never did. That is no credit to me, but much credit to my father. He was authentic through and through. As a kid, I saw and heard the same man in the pulpit on Sunday that I knew at home day after day.

Having graduated from high school, I headed for Ashland College, graduating with a Bachelor of Arts degree in 1965. Though I was uncertain regarding my call to pastoral ministry, I enrolled as a pre-seminary student. During my freshman year, the Lord confirmed my call. Following graduation from Ashland Theological Seminary in 1968, I pastored the Pleasant View Brethren church in Vandergrift, PA. I served four years (1975-1979) as Director of Home Missions and Evangelism for the Missionary Board of the Brethren Church. Since August 1979 I have served as Senior Pastor of Park Street Brethren Church in Ashland, Ohio. In 1983 I completed a Doctor of Ministry degree at Fuller Theological Seminary, with an emphasis on church growth.

My wife, Bobbi (Roberta), is another gracious gift of the Lord to my life. She deeply loves the Lord and has fully supported and participated in the call to pastoral ministry. She also had a full-time career as an elementary teach in the public schools. We have three sons, all now married, graduated from university, and serving the Lord while camouflaged as a systems engineer, a district manager for an insurance company, and a banker. We have three terrific daughters-in-law and eight super grandchildren!

While in pastoral ministry, I have written, in addition to several articles, the exposition and application sections for the Brethren Adult Sunday School Quarterly. I have also authored a book, The Gospel According to Paul, based on Romans 1-8. This grew out of a two and a half-year series of expository sermons on Romans preached at the Park Street Brethren Church. I have also taught personal evangelism and church growth principles by conducting seminars in many Brethren churches.

For nearly thirty years I served the Missionary Board of the Brethren Church either as a member of the Board or staff hired by the Board. Many of those years I served as the President of the Board. I have also served several years on the Executive Board of The Brethren Church, Inc. I served as Moderator of the General Conference of the Brethren Church (1984-1985). In the Ashland community I have served in various roles including membership on the Board of the American Red Cross and the Advisory Board of the Salvation Army.

My goal: to be a life-long learner, not only to acquire head knowledge, but, more importantly, to be a life-long follower of Jesus Christ, to experience His LIFE and to be used of Him, by His Spirit and through the Scriptures, to minister His LIFE, love and grace into the lives of people.

BOB GROVER

Bob grew up in southern New York State as a United Methodist preacher's son. Graduating from Dickinson College in 1975, he married his high school sweetheart, Mary, in December of that year.

Bob attended farrier school in the fall of 1977, and spent 22 years as a full-time farrier in Northern Ohio. When he entered Ashland Theological Seminary, he cut back to part time work. His farrier career included shoeing at Northfield Park, doing therapeutic work for ten years as consulting farrier to the College of Veterinary Medicine at OSU, and teaching farrier science at Otterbein College for 7 years. Occasionally he lectured the OSU veterinary students. Also to his credit he has participated in four American Association of Equine Practitioners— American Farrier's Association sponsored student short courses for veterinary schools. As a member of the AFA for twenty-two years, he served a two-year term as treasurer, was journey certified in 1982, and spent ten years as an examiner and member of the AFA Certification Committee.

Bob has served the Lord in church as a member of the Medina United Methodist Church for 22 years. During that time he served in

189

various leadership positions including: chair of Staff Parish Relations and Worship committees, Lay leader, Administrative Council chair, adult Sunday School teacher, worship leader, and men's Bible study leader. He was called to and certified as a ministry candidate in the UMC in the winter of 2000, and came over to the Brethren denomination in the winter of 2001.

Bob is still working part time as a farrier, attending seminary part time and pastoring a core group of families who planted a new church in Medina, Ohio in the summer of 2000. New Hope Christian Fellowship was chartered as a mission ministry of the Brethren Church in May of 2001.

Bob and Mary, have resided in Lodi, Ohio for 22 years. They have two boys: Eric, 19, an incoming freshman transfer to Ashland University and Ben 21, a junior at Yale. They also have two Jack Russell terriers and a black lab to keep things stirred up a home!

LARITA M. HAND

Rev. Larita M. Hand is the founder and Executive Director of Mercy Missions Inc. located in Cleveland, Ohio. The mission of the non-profit organization is to minister the gospel of Jesus Christ through pastoral counseling, mentoring, discipleship, spiritual retreats and conferences. The outreach component of the organization ministers to the brokenhearted, families in crisis and training for short-term missions to the nations.

Rev. Larita Hand obtained a Bachelors of Arts and Science Degree in 1981 Specialized in Social Work at Cleveland State University, Cleveland, Ohio. She completed the Pastoral Psychology and Counseling Program at Ashland Theological Seminary in 199a. She received a Masters of Divinity Degree in 1998, Drew Theological School, Madison, New Jersey. She is currently pursuing Candidacy for the Doctor of Ministry Degree, Ashland Theological Seminary, Ashland Ohio. She studied abroad in Puerto Rico and Israel.

Rev. Larita Hand was called to ministry in 1985 and licensed the first evangelist in Second Bethlehem Baptist Church in 1986. She then formed the Women's Coffee Hour Prayer Group. This group was interdenominational. Rev. Hand's passion for cross-cultural ministry led her to do short-term missions in China, Philippines, Australia, New

190

Zealand, Zimbabwe, (South Africa), England, North Carolina and New York.

In 1992, Rev. Larita Hand and her family became missionaries to Brooklyn, New York. She was trained how to develop missionary teams and Pastoral Ministry through the African Methodist Church in New York. She was the team leader for mission to Jamaica, West Indies, Ghana West Africa, Trinidad, West Indies, Kenya, East Africa, Nigeria, and West Africa.

Rev. Larita Hand was ordained Deacon 1997 and Itinerant Elder 1998 in the African Methodist Church. She served as Associate Pastor at Macedonia AME Church for three years. She is currently co-pastoring with her husband, Rev. Willie Hand, Faith Christian Fellowship of Ohio in Columbus, Ohio.

Rev. Larita Hand hosted Mercy Missions Inc., International Leadership Conference 2001 in Cleveland, Ohio. The delegates came from Ghana, West Africa, Nigeria West Africa and missionaries from Zimbabwe, South Africa.

SENATOR BILL HARRIS

Senator Harris graduated from the University of Arizona with Honors in Secondary Education and has an Honorary Doctor of Laws Degree from Ashland University. He was a U.S. Marine Corps Major (Enlisted-1953, Commissioned, 1961) and retired from the Marine Corps February 1, 1977 after serving 23 years and 9 months.

While serving in the Marine Corps, Bill served as the Marine Corps Representative, U.S. Army Intelligence School, U.S. Army Intelligence Representative on National Intelligence Board and U.S. Military Representative to the Chief, Vietnam Police Special Branch and received numerous valor, personal and meritorious decorations.

Ohio Senate committees include: Reference—Chairman, Finance and Financial Institutions—Vice Chair, Education—Vice Chair, Agriculture and Rules. Commission appointments include: Controlling Board, Ohio School Facilities Commission, Joint Legislative Ethics Committee, Legislative Committee on Education Oversight.

Bill and his wife, Mary have eleven grown children and fifteen grandchildren.

MARY KAUFMANN

Mary Kaufmann is a Director in Sales Development for The Longaberger Company. Her responsibilities include helping develop and implement Company initiatives that will strengthen relationships between the Company and various audiences, including Longaberger Sales Associates and customers. Her primary function is liaison to the council of Longaberger Independent Sales Directors®.

Kaufmann first joined Longaberger in 1996, where she led the Customer Service Teams. From there she moved to Longaberger University in 1998, where she developed a customer service training program for 700 employees to prepare for the opening of Longaberger Homestead®, as well as designed and facilitated performance-improvement strategies throughout different areas of the Company.

Prior to joining Longaberger, Mary spent nine years with Ameritech, where she was the Director of Customer Service.

Kaufmann graduated in 1987 from Muskingum College with a degree in Computer Science and Business. She obtained her MBA from Baldwin Wallace College in 1990. Mary is currently in pursuit of a Masters of Divinity degree at Ashland Theological Seminary.

She resides in Dresden, Ohio, with her husband Brad, and their two children, Emily and William.

PHIL KIZZEE

Phil has been married for over 18 years and he and his wife have two teenage boys. They enjoy being together and love being supportive parents of active high school student athletes.

His education includes a Bachelor of Arts in Church Music and Christian Education, Olivet Nazarene University and a Master of

Divinity, concentration in Religious Education, Nazarene Theological Seminary.

Rev. Kizzee has served for over fifteen years as a staff pastor in four different Nazarene congregations in Mundelein, Illinois; Beavercreek, Ohio; Chicago, Illinois; Columbus, Ohio. These are small to medium churches ranging in attendance from 175-550. His role at these churches has always included music and worship, with the remained of his duties in administration, education, lay ministry and/or assimilation. He has also served as Interim Pastor in three of these congregations.

His spiritual gifts are administration, creative arts and leadership. His passion is to help lead people in connecting with God (worship) and finding fulfillment in ministry. He has learned much from the staff pastors he has had the opportunity to work with. Phil believes that each situation has helped bring him to be the person and pastor that he is today.

Phil was raised in a Nazarene parsonage and counts it a privilege to have learned ministry from caring and compassionate parents. He feels formal training is a necessity, but believes he has learned a great deal prior to college and seminary, and states that the learning curve kept climbing ever since.

CHARLES LAKE

Dr. Lake is the founding pastor of the Community Church of Greenwood. This is a unique 25-year old congregation that ministers in the Greenwood, Indiana community as an independent, interdenominational church. Sunday morning attendance averages 15-1600. The church has ten daughter congregations, nine in the Greenwood area and one in Lexington, Kentucky. The first daughter church has, in turn, planted five congregations in the Indianapolis area and five in the country of Brazil.

In addition to his pastoral duties, Dr. Lake serves as an Adjunct Professor at Anderson School of Theology, Bethel College Graduate School in Mishawaka, Indiana, Northwest Graduate School of the Ministry, and at the Indianapolis extension of Trinity Evangelical Divinity School. He is a former Board member of the Greater Greenwood Chamber of Commerce, the Board of Trustees of OMS

International, the Board of Trustees of Overseas Council for Theological Education, the Board of Administration of the National Association of Evangelicals, and served as President of the Greenwood Ministerial Association. He also served as a member of the Indianapolis Mayor's Task Force for Family and Neighborhood Projects and the Board of Trustees of African Leadership. He formerly served as Chairman of the Board of Directors of the Indianapolis Care Center and participated in the merger of that ministry with Wheeler Mission Ministries on whose Board of Trustees he now serves. He chaired the White River Township Growth and Development Task Force and served on the Board of the Fellowship of Collegiate Christians. He was Vice-chairman of the Executive Committee for the '99 Indiana Billy Graham Crusade.

Prior to becoming Pastor at CCG, Dr. Lake served for nine years with OMS International, an interdenominational faith mission with World Headquarters in Greenwood. During that ministry he served one year in Australia and spoke extensively in the countries of New Zealand, British Isles, South Africa and Canada. Before coming to OMS he served for eight years as Pastor of the World Gospel Church in Terre Haute, Indiana, a church known for its outstanding missions emphasis.

Presently the overseas missions program of Community Church has an annual budget that exceeds a half a million dollars. He is involved annually in overseas speaking engagements that have included national pastor's conferences, missionary retreats and church dedications.

Dr. Lake holds the following degrees: an AB from Asbury College; an M.Div from Asbury Theological Seminary; and MA from Butler University; a D.Min from Asbury Theological Seminary.

Dr. Lake and his wife, Vicki, presently reside in Greenwood. They have two daughters, Kim Gale (an accountant in Greenwood) and Kara (a Senior at Butler University studying Pre-Med).

C. JAY MATTHEWS

C. Jay Matthews is currently serving in team ministry with his wife, Jacquelyn D. Matthews, as the Senior Pastors of the Mount Sinai Baptist Church. Mount Sinai is celebrating in 2002, seventy-five years of service to God. Mount Sinai Ministries, the Faith Based Agency of Mount Sinai Baptist Church, has become the largest minority, Faith-

194

Based organization, in the city of Cleveland, and one of the largest in the state of Ohio.

His educational background includes a B.A., Malone College, M.A., Ashland Theological Seminary, M.Div., Ashland Theological Seminary, D.Min Candidate Ashland Theological Seminary.

C. Jay is becoming recognized as one of the leaders of faith based activity in our state and within our nation. Mount Sinai Ministries provided several, much needed, services to the community. They include: child Care, Job Development, Job Training, Job Placement, Before and After School Programs, Juvenile Intervention and Prevention Services, Day Treatment, Bridge School, Alternative School, Youth After Care for Youth Returning from Incarceration, Tutoring and Mentoring Programs for youth.

Pastor C. Jay has also developed the Mount Sinai Development Corporation that consists of three housing corporations and a business incubator. They have developed sixty units of housing for senior adults at a cost of 4.2 million dollars. They are currently working to build a multi-plex facility what will include: a Charter School, grades K-8, a high school size gymnasium, a theater, banquet facility, child enrichment/day care center, along with administrative space for the church.

Mount Sinai Baptist Church and Mount Sinai have a combined staff of more than seventy people with fifty being full time. It is a desire of Pastor C. Jay and Jacquelyn D. Matthews to be a catalyst for the redevelopment of this urban community where God has placed their ministry.

He is married with four children and two grandchildren.

SANFORD C. MITCHELL

The Rev. Dr. Sanford C. Mitchell (Sandy), Senior Pastor (since 1979) of Trinity Lutheran church, Ashland, Ohio, graduated from Mansfield (Ohio) Senior High School. He received a B.A. in History from Wittenberg University. After study at the University of South Carolina and the Lutheran Theological Southern Seminary, he received a Master of Divinity from manna School of Theology and a Master of Arts in American History from Bowling Green State University. He received an honorary doctorate (D.D.) from Ashland Theological Seminary, an 800-student seminary in Ashland, Ohio.

Pastor Mitchell served First Lutheran, Findlay and Zion's Lutheran, Defiance before coming to Ashland. He has served for 14 years on the Professional Leadership Unit of the Ohio Synod, as adjunct professor of homiletics at Ashland Theological Seminary and a professor of homiletics for the seminary consortium's Doctor of Ministry program at Methesco Seminary in Worthington, Ohio.

Pastor Mitchell served for nine years as Pastor/Evangelist of the Lutheran Church in America and for four years as Partner in Evangelism in the Evangelical Lutheran Church in America. He is also former editor of the clergy journal, "Homiletics", which provides weekly sermon helps for the Unified Lectionary Series. He served on the Wittenberg Board of Directors for fourteen years.

Pastor and Mrs. Mitchell (Judy) have two sons. Jeffrey is a lay associate for the Lutheran Church. Rodney is head of sales and marketing for Hydromatic Pumps of Ashland.

Pastor Mitchell enjoys fishing and water-skiing in the summertime. In the winter he enjoys cutting wood for his wood-burning furnace that he uses to heat his home. He enjoys volleyball and plays a variety of musical instruments. He has played with folk and bluegrass groups in all of his congregations.

SHAWN OLIVER

Shawn Oliver presently serves as Director of Curriculum and Academic Support Services at Ashland Theological Seminary in Ashland, Ohio. She graduated from Ashland Theological Seminary with a Master of Divinity degree in June 2001. During her final year in seminary, Shawn worked with the Academic Dean's office on the redesign of the Master of Divinity degree program. In her present employment, Shawn also serves as Director of the Master of Divinity program and continues to oversee its redesign.

A native Mississippian, Shawn moved to Ohio in 1993 to pursue her Master of Science degree at The Ohio State University. For her master's thesis, she addressed "Ethical Issues in Agricultural Communication." Upon completion of her degree, she served on a church staff for two and a half years in the role of ministry coordinator. Shawn then worked part time for a corporation in Columbus, Ohio while attending Ashland Seminary. She presently co-teaches a Sunday School class at a local church where she helps people identify and break down barriers to their spiritual growth and relationship with God. Shawn also serves as a retreat speaker for various women" groups.

KHUSHWANT KAUR SIDHU PITTENGER

Dr. Khushwant Kaur Sidhu Pittenger is a naturalized American citizen and considers herself to be an "Ohioan." She was born in India but has live in Ohio for the last twenty years. She has been teaching at Ashland University since 1987. Currently she is a Professor of Business Administration and the Chair of Undergraduate Business Program in the University's College of Business and Economics. She earned her Ph.D. in Business Administration from the University of Cincinnati and MBA in Business Management from Miami University, Oxford, Ohio. Her other degres are from Punjab University, Chadigarh, India.

Her research interests relate to leadership and mentoring. She has presented papers at various national and regional management conferences and has published over a dozen papers. She consults with area businesses on issues related to management training and development. She resides in Ashland, Ohio with her husband and son.

BILL PERKINS

Bill Perkins is the founder and president of the Million Mighty Men. He pastored for over twenty years and has authored numerous books, including: *When Good Men Are Tempted, Fatal Attractions . . . Overcoming Our Secret Addictions* and, *Awaken the Leader Within.* Bill also wrote the New Testament notes for the *Promise Keepers Men's Study Bible* and was one of three contributors to the *Leadership Bible.*

Bill has spoken at Promise Keepers rallies, appeared on nationally broadcast television and radio shows and serves on the faculty for *Man in the Mirror.* He addresses audiences across the country and conducts leadership seminars for companies such as Domino's Pizza and Alaska Airlines.

197

He enjoys working out with his sons and scuba diving. Bill has been meeting with men in small groups for—well, he said it was a long time—like thirty years.

Bill and his wife, Cindy, have three sons and they live in West Linn, Oregon.

S. ROBERT ROSA

Robert (Bob) graduated from Evangel University with a degree in Psychology in 1984. In 1992 he earned two Master of Arts degrees, one in Biblical Studies and the second in Pastoral Counseling from Ashland Theological Seminary. Currently, he is a Doctor of Ministry candidate at Ashland Theological Seminary.

From 1984-1989, Bob served as Program Director at the Toronto Teen Challenge Center, a treatment center for drug and alcohol dependency. For one year, beginning in1988, in Toronto, he was the co-host of Breakthrough, a late night television program providing counseling and encouragement to callers. He served as Hospice Chaplin in Ashland, Ohio from 1990-1992. In 1992, he began as Associate Pastor at Bethel Gospel Tabernacle (Hamilton, Canada and served there until 1996. During this time, his focus was on counseling, family ministries and small group development. Bob served as Senior Pastor at Richland Church of the Brethren (Mansfield, Ohio) from 1997-2000. In 1996, Bob accepted the position of Director of Student Life at Ashland Theological Seminary and continues in that capacity at this time.

Bob received the Outstanding Student Leader Award in 1992 from Ashland Theological Seminary. He served as a committee member on the pastoral Care and Restoration Committee for the Pentecostal Assemblies of Canada, 1993-1996 and the Ministerial Ordination with the Assemblies of God, Ohio.

Bob and Susan have been married for 20 years and have two teenage sons.

RICK RYDING

Rick Ryding is Professor of Christian Education at Mount Vernon Nazarene College. His experience includes staff work at Bethany First, Seattle First and Nashville First Churches of the Nazarene, and a faculty position as Associate Professor of Ministry at Trevecca Nazarene College. He also served as a Missionary, establishing the Nazarene Bible College in Lusaka, Zambia, Africa. Rick holds a Doctor of Education degree in Leadership and Human Resource Development from George Peabody College of Vanderbilt University.

Rick and his wife Bonnie, a counselor in private practice, founded Chestnut Ridge Retreat Center in 1993. "The Ridge" is a part of ServantCare, Inc., an international team ministry of spiritual formation, personnel assessment, training, and counseling for missionaries, ministers, and other Kingdom servants.

Rick and Bonnie have two adult children, Amy and Jeremy.

PAUL A SEARS

Paul Sears is Dean of the College of Business and Economics at **Ashland University** in Ashland Ohio. He also holds the *Mitchell Chair in Administration and Economics*. Prior to his appointment in 1997, he was associate professor of Business Administration and former director of the MBA Program and Coordinator of Graduate Programs at Baldwin-Wallace College, in Berea, Ohio. He is also the former holder of Baldwin-Wallace's *George Herzog Chair in Free Enterprise*.

Paul's prior degree work includes a Ph.D. in Organizational Behavior at Case Western Reserve University; an MBA (Finance and International Business) from the University of Chicago; a Master of Science (Economics) from the London School of Economics, University of London; and undergraduate degrees in Accounting and Economics from Lake Erie College and Yale University.

He has taught at the college level in both California and Ohio, and for the past 20 years has presented seminars on management and finance nationwide and in several foreign countries.

Before entering the academic world full-time, Paul was with the International Banking Department of the First National Bank of Chicago for five years, with assignments in Chicago, London, Los Angeles and San Francisco. He has served as a consultant and trainer for a wide variety of organizations and industries, including **health care** (The Cleveland Clinic, Health Cleveland, Columbia St. John West Shore Hospital, Massillon Community Hospital, VA hospitals, etc.); **banking** (The Federal Reserve Bank of Cleveland, KeyCorp, Bank One, National City Bank, etc.); **manufacturing companies** (Ford Motor Company, M.A. Hanna, Lubrizol, Rubbermaid, RELTEC, Lumitex, Creative Arts Activities, etc.) and **service organizations** (Domino's Pizza, GE Information Systems, Cuyahoga County Treasurer's Office, Cuyahoga County Library System, etc.,). Prior to moving to Ohio, Paul was one of the founding partners of the Berkeley Consulting Group based in the San Francisco, California, area.

Paul lives in Ashland with his wife, Odette, two sons (Michale, age 12; Nicholas, age 6) and daughter (Olivia, age 3).

BEVERLY BEDWELL SPRENG

Beverly Bedwell Spreng is a native of Kettering, Ohio and was raised in a family of four girls. She attended Miami University in Oxford, Ohio and graduated with a Bachelor of Science Degree in Consumer Science with teaching certification in the field. Immediately following graduation, she married Mike Spreng, from Ashland, Ohio, and moved directly to North Carolina, where Mike attend dental school at the University of North Carolina in Chapel Hill. While in Chapel Hill, Bev was employed by the Chief Medical Examiners office for the state and assisted with the creation of a state-wide child abuse and neglect program, recruiting and contracting with physicians in each county of the state to examine children suspected of being abused and/or neglected. In 1980 Mike and Bev moved back to Ashland so Mike could join his father's dental practice. Between 1980 and 1989, Bev and Mike had two children and Bev worked as a substitute teacher, a receptionist and an aerobics instructor.

In 1989 Bev's career focus changed to adult vocational education. She served as Transition Coordinator at Ashland County West Holmes Career Center and at Madison Adult Education in Mansfield, Ohio. In 1995, Bev "retired" to spend more time with her growing children. She soon discovered that keeping up with two busy teens could be a full time job. In 1998 Bev graduated from Leadership Ashland, a community leadership training program, that precipitated her involvement on several community boards including Mental Health and Recovery Board and Ashland Community Arts Center Board. She is also active on various school related advisory councils and committees and is a member of the Ashland City Board of Education. In July of 2001, Bev became the Executive Director of Leadership Ashland. Through her community involvement, she has discovered how important it is for every citizen to do their part to keep our community viable and strong and to ensure that our youth are provided the education, guidance, acceptance and love they need to become productive, respectful, responsible and caring citizens.

VICKIE TAYLOR

Vickie Taylor, M. Div., is Director of Technology Resources at Ashland Theological Seminary in Ashland, Ohio. She came to Ashland as a second career student. Her first career was as a business manager for nonprofits. As a business manager, she was responsible for personnel as well as the finances of the business.

After having come to Ashland to earn her Master of Divinity Degree, she became involved in the area of Church leadership and Church Administration as the graduate assistant to Dr. Leroy Solomon, professor of Church Leadership. Upon graduation from seminary she was hired to assist the seminary in the development of technology in teaching and learning as well as teaching technology to future leaders in the church.

Vickie also serves as a member of the leadership team at University Church in Ashland and is a small-group pastor. She has been married to her husband, Bob, for the last 23 years and they have an 18-year old son.

LOVETT H. WEEMS, JR.

Dr. Lovett H. Weems, Jr., is President of Saint Paul School of Theology in Kansas City, Missouri. Prior to coming to Saint Paul, he served as Vice President of Wesley Theological Seminary in Washington, D.C., and before that, as a local church pastor for eighteen years.

As President of Saint Paul, Dr. Weems has focused on improving the quality of congregational leadership. As Professor of Church Leadership, Dr. Weems teaches future leaders of the church. His book *Church Leadership*, published by Abingdon Press, has been described by Professor Rosabeth Moss Kanter of Harvard University as "an invaluable guide to leadership in the church." Beyond Saint Paul, Dr. Weems lectures and speaks frequently at colleges, universities, and denominational events, as well as preaching often at Annual Conferences and convocations.

A native of Mississippi, Dr. Weems is a graduate of Millsaps College; Perkins School of Theology, Southern Methodist University; and Wesley Theological Seminary.

In 1989 he was inducted into the John Wesley Society, which honors the outstanding graduates of Wesley Theological Seminary. In 1997 Baker University awarded him the honorary Doctor of Divinity degree.

His years in local church ministry in Mississippi were marked by emphasis on evangelism, mission, church school, and social concerns. His work in Mississippi led the distinguished Mississippi writer Willie Morris to describe him as "one of the persons who added much to the growing civility of Mississippi."

Dr. Weems is the author of over 200 articles and reviews in national publications, as well as several books. His latest book is *Leadership in the Wesleyan Spirit*. His book *John Wesley's Message Today,* also published by Abingdon Press, is used throughout the denomination as a study book for laity and clergy on Wesleyan theology. Russian and Indonesian editions have been published.

He and his wife, Emily, a public school teacher, are the parents of four children.

The Sandberg
Leadership Center

On the Campus of Ashland Theological Seminary

Don't do what the world needs
Do what keeps you alive;
For what the world needs
Is you, alive!
--Howard Thurman

The Sandberg Leadership Center is located on the Campus of Ashland Theological Seminary. From the heart of northeast Ohio, the center serves the growing need for quality leadership training throughout the United States.

Our Mission

We are a center of transformational learning, committed to the spiritual and character formation of servant leaders who will make a difference in business, government, church, and society.
- *We practice transformational learning:* Transformational leaning produces reflective leaders of integrity, courage and wisdom.
- *We commit to spiritual and character formation:* Leaders express clear, personal core values in competencies consistent with good leadership.
- *We believe servant leaders make a difference:* Leadership is the ability to get things done. Servant leadership accomplishes tasks by investing in people.
- *We serve leaders in business, government, church, and society:* The Center will focus on developing leadership in business, government, church, and society.

Our Values

The Sandberg Leadership Center is committed to a biblical understanding of life, education, and ministry:
- We value **servant leadership** as the biblical model
- We value **spiritual formation** that results in life renewed and the recovery of identity in Christ.
- We value **self-understanding** and **discovery**.

203

- We value **team building** and shared responsibility within the organization.
- We value the vision of the leader as a **change agent** in the organization and society.
- We value the **redemption, personal healing** and **equipping** of each participant.
- We value an attitude of **stewardship** and careful **discernment of the culture**.

Seeing the Future

The decades of changing culture have shaken the foundations of business, government and the church. The older ways of management treat the church, business, and government as machines. The new paradigm, formed through servant leadership, views organization in personal images of teams, networks and partners or in biblical images of "family," "body" and "living stones."

Throughout the culture is the cry for leaders But, it is not necessarily a cry for more leaders, or better leaders, but a cry for a different king of leader: one who is empowered by the synergy of servant leadership and spiritual formation for renewing the organization.

Such a leader is competent in two skills: The forming one's self as a servant leader, and the forming of the organization as servant people. This leader is equipped to move the organization toward a system of relationship and empowerment. It is our purpose at The Sandberg Leadership Center to model the new paradigm as we provide transformational learning for Christian Leaders in business, government and the church.

Contact Us

If we can serve you in leadership training; if you would like information on programs available for you and your organization; or if you would like to know how you can participate in the development of The Sandberg Leadership Center, contact us at:

The Sandberg Leadership Center
910 Center Street
Ashland, Ohio 44805
1-419-289-5323

Richard Leslie Parrott, Ph.D.
Executive Director
April 2, 2000

RICHARD LESLIE PARROTT, PH.D.

Dr. Parrott is the Executive Director of The Sandberg Leadership Center in Ashland, Ohio. The Center is dedicated to Transformational Leadership in business, government and the church. Dr. Parrott has worked collaboratively with leadership centers at Yale Divinity School, Claremont School of Theology, and the Gordon-Conwell School of Theology.

Richard Leslie Parrott is also the Director of the Doctor of Ministry Program at Ashland Theological Seminary in Ashland, Ohio. Dr. Parrott works with over one hundred pastors from twenty-five denominations and many world areas. His teaching in the doctoral program includes course work in Transformational Leadership including: *"Political Reality and Spiritual Leadership," "Organizing for Spiritual Renewal,"* and *"Leading Profound Change."*

He was educated at Eastern Nazarene College (B.A.), University of Missouri (M.A. in Psychology), Nazarene Theological Seminary (M.Div.), and received his Ph.D. from Oregon State University in Education Administration. He has further education from the Executive School of University of Michigan in Ann Arbor Michigan.

He has guided both boards and individuals in pursuit of Leadership Excellence at the Strategic Leadership Conference in Seattle, WA, the Ohio State Board of Pharmacy, the Ohio Chamber of Commerce, Values-Based Impact for Non-Profits in San Francisco, CA, and the Lilly Leadership Grant program on Non-Profit Organizations at Yale University. Dr. Parrott is a resident of Ashland, Ohio where he is an active participant in the community. He is on the board of the Chamber of Commerce and Leadership Ashland.

Dr. Parrott speaks extensively. His duties include faculty participation in Church Planting Seminars and Church Health and Renewal Seminars. He consults with business and faith-based organizations. He is a frequent speaker for conferences, seminars and special events.

Dr. Parrott is married to Shirley and they have five grown children; Kurtis, Andrew, LeAnne, Robert, and Justin. The Parrotts reside in Ashland, Ohio.